tim.dowle82@gmail.com

ISBN 9781077432239

Dedicated to all those from or connected to the Goytre area who served or otherwise contributed during the Great War 1914-1918, no matter the magnitude of their service

Contents

Acknowledgements

This book would not have been possible without the help of many people: firstly my parents, Richard and Elaine Dowle, for their extensive contribution to the painstaking tasks of identifying historical addresses, general map work, photography and multiple proof readings.

Secondly, thanks to Mike Jones, a fellow armed forces veteran of Goytre and lately the Gwent Poppy Appeal Co-ordinator, who originally suggested turning my idea into an exhibition and then a publication. Mike, along with his wife Angela, remain instrumental in village commemorations, including the placement of the Silent Soldier statue and the planting of poppies, grown from seed brought back from Flanders field (pictured below)

Thirdly, to anyone who contributed either stories, photographs or simply encouragement to complete this project. Significant contributions have come from Jane and Jeff Phillips for their information on Saron Chapel and the Morgan family, David Owen and Alan Otton for their immense local knowledge and photograph collection and also Brenda Harris, one of Goytre's last links to the Great War, whose parents both served. Brenda shared her memories and photographs for this project but sadly passed away prior to publication.

Finally, I would like to thank my wife and children for their patience and support during this project.

Also, here is the right place to offer apologies in relation to any misinformation or individuals missing from this work, which is purely unintentional and down to the fact that they simply have not featured in any of the sources I have consulted.

Introduction

I regularly make the 50-mile drive from my current home in Gloucestershire back to Goytre where I spent the first eighteen years of my life. Often choosing to forgo the grey monotony of the motorways, I prefer the longer but greener and certainly more picturesque drive through the Forest of Dean. Passing through the small villages, one can often spot small but well cared for war memorials on village greens or within the grounds of the churches that lie next to the road, that remember the fallen and sometimes even the survivors of the Great War, Second World War and other conflicts of past generations.

In 2018, with the 100th anniversary commemorations of the end of the Great War approaching and with the steady flow of media coverage, I reflected on the question of how Goytre remembers its war dead, or if indeed Goytre was perhaps a Thankful Village (Pentrefi Diolchgar in Welsh) where all who served came home?

A quick check of the Commonwealth War Graves Commission website revealed that sadly Goytre was not a Thankful Village but from personal experience I knew that Goytre did not have what might be termed a 'traditional' war memorial. However, further investigation revealed that there are memorials in Goytre, all sited within places of worship, namely St Peter's Church, Saron Baptist Chapel and Capel Ed. I had a vague recollection of two plaques in Capel Ed, having been a member of the Youth Club that meets there, but I had hardly been inside St Peter's since my christening and had never been to the Saron Chapel.

This then raised a problem in my mind. Many locals who have simply by circumstance not had reason to visit these locations would be unaware of these memorials and, in what was meant to be a year of remembrance, the sacrifices made by villagers would be overlooked.

I raised my concerns with my parent's neighbour, a former soldier, retired senior police officer and now stalwart of the Royal British Legion and he agreed with me. The result of this conversation was a plan to host a memorial exhibition in the Goytre Arms on 29th September 2018, the 100th anniversary of the death in action of Frederick Pinfield who had been born at Goytre Hall.

What followed was months of intense research covering census returns, individual service files of personnel from all branches of the armed forces, examination of unit war diaries and the accumulation of countless local maps and the interviewing of several of Goytre's oldest residents.

The event was well-attended and covered by the South Wales Argus in their special WW1 commemorative edition. The spectrum of visitors ranged from members of the local scout group, who were undertaking their own WW1 project, to relatives of those who had served and were included in the exhibition material. The centre piece was a large map of Goytre on which were plotted the residences of all those identified as serving, along with a brief summary of their service and fate.

The exhibition had been intended to be the conclusion of my work. However, following the event I had the feeling that there was unfinished business and, in the words of Winston Churchill, it was simply the "end of the beginning". My primary concern was that the exhibition was a one off and still didn't solve the problem of a permanent and publicly visible memorial. Also, more information had come to light, including the discovery of several more locals who had served and I had previously missed.

The next stage was the launch of a website to publish and make publicly available the stories of those who served and to act as an online war memorial; it also provided a portal for people to submit further information should they have it. The information from the website was then used by the Goytre Scout Group, who for the Armistice Day commemorations created large poppies for each of the 22 local fallen. These were attached to lamp posts around the village, creating a Poppy Trail. Each poppy contained a tag with the details of the individual it commemorated, along with a scannable image that when read by a mobile phone would take the user straight to the web page giving a full biography. Another positive from the research was that it enabled the full names of the war dead to be read out at St

Peter's at their 11th November service for the first time, rather than just initials.

The motivation for this book is to go beyond the scope of the website and take a more holistic view of Goytre in the Great War, including the area's involvement on the Home Front through fundraising and agricultural endeavours.

Finally, as the objective of this book is to explore the experiences of Goytre and its inhabitants during the Great War I have deliberately stayed away from political and military commentary; these subjects are covered in depth in numerous other publications.

Goytre

Goetre, Goytre, Goytrey - Over the years the name of this area has had many spellings. These derived from the original Welsh name of Coed Tre, the settlement in the forest. This was a hamlet near Ty Cooke farm, Mamhilad, which was wiped out by the plague.[1] A description of the parish in William Coxe's (1747-1828) 1801 publication 'An Historical Tour Through Monmouthshire' states: 'The hamlet of Goytre or Coedtrev in the midst of the region, derives its appellation from the forests with which it is surrounded, and abounds with delightful recesses and pleasant glades dotted with white cottages'.

Early photograph of the Carpenter's Arms, now the Goytre Arms

---

[1] From the Goytre Community Council website http://www.community-council.org.uk/goetrefawr/

The electoral area today is termed Goetre Fawr but the name Goytre is commonly used for both the area and also the village of Penperlleni (and this terminology has been used in this book). The latter name is thought by some to derive from the welsh word Perllan, meaning an orchard, but it seems more likely to be from the place name Pelleny or Pellenny, as documented in ancient leases in the parish of Goytrey.

The centre piece of the armistice 100th anniversary exhibition, held at the Goytre Arms in September 2018, was a large-scale map of the area showing the residences of the men from the Goytre area who served in WW1.

A modern map was used, at a scale of 6 inch to the mile, which delineated the boundary of the present Goetre Fawr Community Council. This council was known at the time of WW1 as the Parish of Goytrey or Goytre. Comparing the modern council's boundary with an Ordnance Survey map of the early 20th century shows, perhaps surprisingly, that the boundary has remained virtually unchanged.

Junction of Star Road and School Lane, early 20th century. The Old Smithy is on the far right of the row of buildings in the background

The council area is approximately in the shape of a quadrangle, being about 3.5 miles east to west and 3.5 miles north to south. Three significant transportation routes run south to north through the area: the Monmouthshire and Brecon Canal, the A4042 Newport to Abergavenny Trunk Road, and the Welsh Marches railway line from Newport to Shrewsbury. The village of Penperlleni is the largest

5

settlement in the area and lies on the trunk road approximately 6 miles south of Abergavenny and 4 miles north of Pontypool.

The council area boundaries are mainly along geographical features, about half being watercourses. The northern boundary includes the Gwenffrwd and Nant Rhyd-y-meirch streams: the northeastern/eastern, the Nant y Robwl and River Usk: the southern, the Nant y Pia and the Berthin Brook: the western, the mountain ridge of Mynydd Garn-wen between the Eastern Valley of the former County of Gwent and the Vale of the River Usk.

The map provided on page 7 shows the extent of Goetre Fawr Community Council. The villages and hamlets of Penperlleni, Llanover, Little Mill, Monkswood, Mamhilad, Nantyderry, Pencroesoped, Penpedairheol and Croes y Pant are marked and are all recorded as residences of WW1 soldiers. The exhibition map showed, as accurately as possible, where individuals were residing or working and demonstrated the total blanket cover of the answer to the call to arms; sometime adjacent houses and farms, sometimes every other house or farm, brothers, even a soldier and his future wife (see p.46/47). This book pays tribute to them all.

All the individuals recorded in this book were either born within the boundaries of the parish or are commemorated on memorials within it, specifically St Peter's Church, Saron Chapel and Capel Ed.

Rose Cottage, Ivy Cottage and Phoenix Cottage, Penperlleni at around the time of the Great War

6

Map

Villages and hamlets of Goetre Fawr

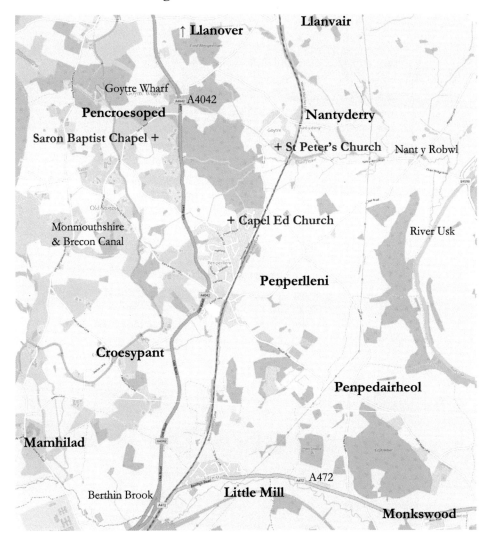

The First To Go

For Great Britain the war began on 4th August 1914, however for the Abergavenny Chronicle it seemed very much to be business as usual. Just three days later an article about a London oyster bar mistreating lobsters was printed on page two, a whole page ahead of any mention of the outbreak of war. Coverage began at the top of the third page including the plea made by Lord Kitchener that day for a further 100,000 volunteers to enlist in the Army.

Goytre's reaction to the outbreak of war is unrecorded, however by the time villagers were reading about London lobsters the first of their friends and neighbours were answering Kitchener's call and those with Reserve commitments or serving as Territorials had departed. Several of them with the local Territorial Regiment, the Monmouthshire's.

Formed in 1908 as part of the Haldane Reforms, which saw the old militia style and volunteer Battalions formed into a new Territorial Force, the Monmouthshire Regiment was rare in that it was comprised wholly of Territorial Battalions whilst most others were affiliated with regular Army Regiments. The common configuration of an Infantry Regiment at the time was a regular battalion serving in the UK, a second regular battalion serving overseas with the third Battalion being Territorial, based in the geographic area the Regiment recruited from.

Within the Monmouthshire Regiment the 1st Battalion was based in Newport, the 2nd in Pontypool and the 3rd in Abergavenny. In addition to these HQ locations there were multiple drill halls, which for the 2nd Battalion included Blaenavon, Crumlin and Llanhilleth. It was at these halls that the Territorials would meet weekly for training.

The Commanding Officer of the 2nd Battalion was Boer War veteran Colonel Edward Cuthbertson of Goytre Hall. The Battalion was mobilised on 5th August and the men left their homes to proceed to their place of muster. Initially posted on home defence duties at Pembroke Dock[1] and then for training at Northampton, the 2nd Mons had the distinction of being one of the first Territorial units in France when it arrived at Le Havre on 7th November 1914.

---

[1] Territorial Units were originally formed for Home Defence. Soldiers had no obligation to serve overseas but the majority signed up for Imperial Service and accepted liability for overseas deployment.

In addition to Colonel Cuthbertson the following Goytre men are known to have arrived in France with the 2nd Mons on that initial date:

Lewis Brown (Croesypant)

James Clark (Little Mill)

Reginald Cornish (Penperlleni)

Henry Guest (Penperlleni)

William Thomas Higgs (Mamhilad)

William Morgan (Penperlleni)

George Skillern (Little Mill)

William Skillern (Little Mill)

Frank Wall (Mamhilad)

Lewis Brown had only just survived a brush with death just months previously on 19th March 1914, in a mining accident which killed two of his colleagues

It is interesting to note that Reginald Cornish '1343', William Higgs '1344' and Henry Guest '1345' had sequential service numbers indicating that they either enlisted together or at least very closely together, which based on their service numbers was in the summer of 1912.[1] Reginald was destined to be the only one of that trio to survive the war.

The Mons Clasp

All the Goytre men who arrived in France with the 2nd Mons on 7th November 1914 became eligible for the 1914 Star medal, the criteria for which was service in France between 5th August and 22/23 November 1914. Reginald Cornish, James Clark and Colonel Cuthbertson are distinguished further in that they also qualified for what became known as the Mons[2] Clasp, awarded to those who between those dates came under fire or were within range of enemy

---

[1] Evidenced by Henry Guest's service record, which has survived.

[2] Referring to the Battle of Mons rather than the abbreviation of Monmouthshire.

artillery. They would have been with either C or D Company of the 2nd Mons, who were the first contingent of the Battalion to enter the trenches, a day before the clasp qualification period ended.

A further distinction for these men was that they were part of the British Army that became to be known as the Old Contempitbles, men of the original British Expeditionary Force who held up the German advance and whom the German Kaiser referred to in an order as "Sir John French's contemptible little army".

As the 2nd Mons began their active service a steady trickle of casualties began, however the first Goytre serviceman to fall was from the 1st Battalion of the King's Shropshire Light Infantry. Sergeant Edward Davies, whose sister Martha Lloyd lived at Nantyderry, was probably either a mobilised reservist or a regular serving soldier at the start of the war. He was killed on 25th October 1914, having arrived in France on 10th September.

The 2nd Monmouthshire Battalion depart from Pontypool, image from the Torfaen Museum Trust collection / casgliad Ymddiriedolaeth Amgueddfa Torfaen

The second Goytre casualty was Henry Guest of Myrtle Cottage, School Lane. Henry was killed during the 2nd Mons second period in the trenches, dying on 11th December 1914, most likely killed by a sniper.

Another early Goytre participant was Jack Davis who enlisted on 10th August for the 1st Battalion Monmouthshire Regiment and arrived in France in March 1915. Just weeks later in early May he was presumed killed in action at the Battle of Frezenberg Ridge, however it soon transpired that it was another soldier of the same Battalion and with the same name who had been killed. This started a chain of events in which Jack's wife had to battle the military authorities for them to accept he was still alive and writing to her weekly from France! He was eventually wounded late in the war, suffering a gunshot to the head but ultimately survived.

From the 3rd Battalion, Monmouthshire Regiment, Reginald Baker and Lionel Digby who both had Goytre connections had also begun their march to the front line.

In addition to those already mentioned the following are also determined as having enlisted within the first months of the war based on their arrival overseas in 1914 or early 1915:

Sidney Bache (Penpedairheol) – Worcestershire Regiment, **Arthur Edward Evans** (Penperlleni) – Royal Field Artillery, **Benjamin Evans** (Upper Llanover) – Welsh Guards, **David Harry** (Pencroesoped) – King's Shropshire Light Infantry, **Phillip Jenkins** (Pencroesoped) – Royal Welsh Fusiliers, **William Jones** (Nantyderry) – Royal Army Medical Corps, **Benjamin Morgan** (Mamhilad) – Royal Field Artillery, **Ira Morgan** (Pontypool) – South Wales Borderers, **Albert Victor Parsons** (Goytre) – Royal Welsh Fusiliers, **Major Phillips** (Glebe Cottage) – Royal Army Medical Corps, **James Smith** (Monkswood) – Royal Engineers, **Arthur Williams** (Mamhilad) – 2nd Mons.

It was not just the armed forces who had mobilised, the effort on the Home Front was also ramping up.

The first evidence of Goytre's effort on the home front comes in the 7th August edition of the Abergavenny Chronicle. Goytre Parish Church is recorded as raising over £17 at its last Sunday services for the National Relief Fund, with £14 being collected at the morning service. Established by Prince Edward in August 1914, the National Relief Fund raised money for the families of serving men, raising over £1million in its first week.

Everywhere across the nation funds and collections were being raised, often by the gentry to support either national initiatives or local regiments.[1] Goytre was no exception, the Abergavenny Chronicle of 6th November 1914 details Mrs Cuthbertson's plea for donations for her husband's regiment of shirts, socks, sweaters, mittens, mufflers or belts in khaki or grey. Money, cigarettes and tobacco were also gratefully received and could be donated at Goytre Hall.

As 1914 drew to a close Goytre was fully immersed in the war both through the military service of locals and increasing efforts on the home front. Over twenty local men are known to have been either at the front or in training at this point, just over a fifth of all those from the area who served. The area had also experienced its first two casualties.

Any early notions of the war being over by Christmas had evaporated as the Western Front degenerated into the stagnant trench warfare that was to become synonymous with the next four years of fighting, during which over a hundred Goytre men served with a fifth of that number killed.

Those Who Served

This chapter details the lives of those from the area who are known to have served and fit the criteria set out a few pages ago, in that they were born or otherwise closely linked to Goytre. Unfortunately, in some cases, primarily due to a lack of a full name or a common surname it has been impossible to positively identify an individual.

It is likely that more than are listed here did serve, however due to the passage of time and the fact that many Great War service records were destroyed or severely fire damaged during the Blitz, these are the only ones that are identifiable.

To identify those who served and piece together their stories a multitude of sources have been reviewed, starting with the Goytre area returns for the Absent Voters List of 1918. The 1916 Representation of the People Act had ruled that those serving overseas and eligible to vote by proxy or post would be recorded on registers, grouped by their

---

[1] 11,407 charities were registered between 1916 and 1920 of which some still exist today including the Royal British Legion and St Dunstan's.

home constituency. The register gives the names, addresses and regimental details of forty-five men from Goytre.

The Absent Voters List was then cross referenced with the census returns of 1891, 1901 and 1911. These list all residents or overnight visitors in the enumeration area on the day the census was taken. Records are grouped by household and record the names, ages, birthplace, current address and occupation of individuals. With the 1921 census not due for release until 2021 and the 1931 census destroyed in an accidental warehouse fire in 1942, the next available source of information is the 1939 Register.

Recorded on 29th September 1939, just weeks into the Second World War, the register was taken to enable the production of National Identity Cards and later Ration Books. Post World War II it was also used as the basis for the National Health Service Register. For the purpose of this book it has provided valuable insight into the lives of our servicemen after they returned from war.

In reaction to increasing public interest in the Great War due to anniversaries, and the broadcast of television programmes such as 'Who Do You Think You Are' prompting a surge in family history research, a vast amount of surviving records have been digitised and made available online by the likes of The National Archives, Ancestry and FindMyPast. These include military service and pension records for all three services which give details of when and where a man enlisted, where he served and any wounds. Medal index cards confirm what medals a soldier was entitled to and on which date they first entered an operational area, providing this date was prior to 1st January 1916. Finally, parish birth, marriage and death records are also available online and provide insight into the key dates of individual's lives.

All those who have been identified are detailed in the following pages, in alphabetical order by surname. Information where known includes where in Goytre they lived and the medals they were awarded for their service. A breakdown of units served in is provided in Appendix C and a description of medals mentioned is given in Appendix D.

Alexander, Frank. Trooper, 39620. 3rd Hussars

Woodland Cottage, Pencroesoped
Queen's South Africa Medal, British War Medal, Victory Medal

Frank Alexander was baptised in Llanfair Kilgeddin on 4th December 1881. He was the son of Railway Labourer Thomas Alexander (b.1849, Wiltshire) and his wife Harriet Prior (b. 1850, Berkshire). The 1881 census shows the family living at Llanvair Cross, Llanfair Kilgeddin. Thomas died in 1883 aged 34 and his widow Harriet married again later the same year, to Warren Sharp (b.1843, Goytre) a Railway Platelayer. By 1901 Frank had left home and was living at Drysiog Farm, Ebbw Vale where he was employed as a Milkman by Farmer Rees Edwards.

By this time the Boer War had been dragging on for over a year. In South Africa many troops were deployed in combat operations, resulting in a lack of resource for policing duties. Baden Powell formulated a plan to recruit up 10,000 men from the British Empire to fill the void. On 12th November 1901, Frank completed an application form for the South African Constabulary (S.A.C), giving his address as Yew Tree Cottage, Llanover and his description as 5ft 8inches tall with a dark complexion, grey eyes and dark brown hair. He listed his mother as next of kin and declared a magistrate's conviction for trespassing in pursuit of hares for which he had been fined 19 shillings. On 26th November he signed the Articles of Agreement and became a 3rd Class Trooper in the S.A.C, signing his Attestation Papers upon arrival in Pretoria in January 1902. From the Depot he was posted to No 10 Troop and joined them on 1st February 1902. The Boers mostly waged a guerrilla style war and the S.A.C. frequently took casualties.

On 12th December 1902 Frank wrote to his Commanding Officer to request his discharge. This was approved with the comment 'he has a guarantee of six months employment in the town, and I recommend his application. He is a good man but will not be any loss as a policeman'.

Frank took his discharge on Christmas Day 1902 after 346 days service and a character assessment of Very Good, giving his address as the Middlebury Imperial Restaurant. For his service Frank was awarded the Queen's South Africa Medal with clasps Cape Colony, Orange Free State, Transvaal and South Africa 1902.

Despite his initial plan to remain in South Africa, Frank returned to Wales and married his wife Annie in the summer of 1904. The 1911 census lists Frank, his wife and two children living at Penyrhoel where he was employed as a Market Gardener.

In 1917 Frank was conscripted for the Army but he lodged an appeal. His case is described in the Abergavenny Chronicle on 31st August 1917:

COUNTY TRIBUNAL. SIR HENRY MATHER-JACKSON AND AGRICULTURAL CASES.

There was only one local case before the County Appeal Tribunal on Monday. This was the case of Frank Alexander, smallholder and market gardener, of Llanover, who has also been working underground as a timber man for the Blaenavon Company. In this case Mr Homfray Davies (secretary of the Monmouthshire Farmers' Union) attempted to get in a word. The Chairman told him he could not hear him. The agricultural question had been taken out of their hands by the Board of Agriculture, and the cases must either go before the War Agricultural Committee or come direct before them. If they came there, notwithstanding Mr. Davies's official appointment by the Board of Agriculture, then they would refuse to hear him, because he had no locus standi. If the Board of Agriculture were not satisfied he would refer the whole of the cases to that body. They could not go on reviewing the cases and hearing anyone who liked to come there. He would continue to hear Mr. Harding as the representative of the agricultural interest, but as a matter of courtesy (he knew nothing officially of any other appointment) he would hear Mr. Davies in any case which had not been before the War Agricultural Committee. The application was refused, the man to join on October 27th.

Frank subsequently served overseas with the 3rd Hussars. He was discharged on 9th February 1919 and was awarded the British War Medal and Victory Medal.

Widowed in early 1933 Frank married again the following year, on 2nd April 1934 at Llangattock Juxta Usk, to Plezze of Bryn Cottage. Frank's address was given as The Lower Hendre, Llanover.

The 1939 register lists Frank and Plezze living at Woodland Cottage, Goytre with Frank employed as a Gardener. He died on 11th February 1947, aged 65. Burial records show that he had been living at Upper Caecoed, Llanover at the time of death and was buried at Llangattock-juxta-Usk.

Andrews, W. C.

Listed as a survivor on the St Peter's church memorial. Possibly Walter Charles Andrews who was born in Bedfordshire in 1895 and married Ethel May Watkin of 'Trinidad', Goytre on 8th August 1925 at St Peter's.

Bache, Sidney James. Private, 1975. Worcestershire Regiment

Royal Oak Cottage, Penpedairheol
1914/15 Star, British War Medal, Victory Medal

Born in Shropshire on 20th October 1882, Sidney entered employment with the Great Western Railway in 1899 and worked his way up from Engine Cleaner to Fireman to Engineman via postings to Chester, Gobowen, Wolverhampton and Newport. On the 1911 census he is listed as living on Alexandra Road, Newport and working as a Locomotive Fireman.

Sidney was injured on 24th January 1912; whilst travelling on the footplate of a locomotive he was knocked off by a bridge and became caught by a wagon, suffering bruising to his head.

On the outbreak of war Sidney joined the Worcestershire Regiment and arrived in France in March 1915 but was later transferred to the Royal Army Medical Corps. He is recorded on the 1918 Absent Voters List as living at Royal Oak Cottages, Goytre.

Sidney was discharged from the Army in April 1919 due to wounds or sickness. Returning to work with the GWR he was employed primarily at Bristol and Swindon. He died at Bristol General Hospital on 2nd February 1940, aged 57.

Baker, Reginald L. Captain, 3rd Battalion Monmouthshire Regiment

Abergavenny
1914/15 Star, British War Medal, Victory Medal

Reginald Lawrence Baker was born in Abergavenny in June 1878 and at the time of the 1881 census was living with his family at Llantilio Pertholey where his father was a Solicitor. Following in his father's footsteps, by 1911 Reginald was also a solicitor and living at 44 Frogmore Street, Abergavenny.

By the outbreak of war Reginald was a Captain in the 3rd Battalion, Monmouthshire Regiment, having served for several years with the Territorial Force and the 4th Volunteer Battalion, South Wales Borderers. He embarked for France in early 1915, just weeks after marrying his wife, Grace Helen Torry in Cambridgeshire where the Battalion were completing their training.

In early May 1915 all three Monmouthshire Regiment Battalions were involved in the fierce fighting at Frezenberg, just outside Ypres where the Germans had launched an advance with the objective of sweeping through to capture the Channel ports. The 3rd Battalion suffered heavy casualties on 8th May, including Captain Baker who was killed in action on that date.

Buried at the Poelcapelle British Cemetery, Reginald is also commemorated on many memorials in the wider Abergavenny area, including at St Peter's church, Goytre.

Bandfield, George. Corporal, 167709. Royal Air Force

Nantyderry Mill
British War Medal, Victory Medal

Born in Llanbadoc, Usk on 3rd April 1888, George is listed on the 1911 census as a Domestic Gardener. A Police Constable by the start of the war he enlisted for Royal Air Force on 15th May 1918, just five weeks after its formation. On enlistment George gave his address as Nantyderry Mill.

Serving as a Driver he arrived in Egypt on 30th July 1918 and remained there until he was processed for discharge in March 1920. Returning to civilian life he married Jessie Bishop in 1928 but died only three years later in 1931, aged 42 whilst living at Goytre Farm. He is buried at St Peter's.

Belcher, W. H.

Listed as survivor on the memorial at St Peter's church he cannot be positively identified on records.

Bowen, Lewis Richard. Sapper, 213542. Royal Engineers

Oak Cottage, Mamhilad
British War Medal, Victory Medal

Lewis Richard Bowen of Oak Cottage, Mamhilad was baptised at St Peter's Church, Goytre on 24th February 1889. Enlisting for the Army at Newport on 12th September 1916, Lewis was posted to the Royal Engineers. He gave his civilian trade as carpenter and listed his employer as Mr D Bowen of Sunny Bank, Mamhilad.

Arriving in France in mid-1917, Lewis was posted to the Durham Light Infantry for two months before it was decided that his skills would be better utilised with the Royal Engineers.

On 8th November 1918 whilst serving with the 61st Field Company and just three days before the end of the war, Lewis was hit in his left foot by machine gun fire. After treatment in the field and at the 53rd General Hospital at Boulogne he was evacuated to the UK on 14th November. Following further treatment at the 3rd Western General Hospital in Neath he was discharged from the Army on 28th February 1919.

In addition to the British War Medal and Victory Medal, Lewis received the Silver War Badge, granted to those discharged from the services as a result of illness or injury. He is recorded on the list of survivors on the memorial plaque in St Peter's.

Lewis died on 5th January 1931 aged 41, shortly after an operation at Pontypool Hospital. Living in Mamhilad at the time of his death he was buried at Mamhilad Church.

Brinkworth, William John. 111685, Private. Tank Corps

Rose Cottage, Little Mill
British War Medal, Victory Medal

Sometimes named in records as John William Brinkworth, he was born in the Pontypool area on 18th March 1898 and is listed on the 1911 census living at Rose Cottage, Little Mill. He attended Mamhilad School, first appearing in the register in 1902.

William commenced employment at Pontypool Road Station in October 1915 as a Cleaner but left in 1916, probably to join the Army. He served in France with the 7th Battalion, Tank Corps and received the British War Medal and Victory Medal.

On the 1939 register William is recorded living at Fowler Street, Pontypool and working in the Steel Sheet Mill. He died in the Pontypool area in 1945, aged 46.

Brown, Arthur. 119654, Private. Royal Flying Corps

Monkswood

Born on 25th April 1891 in Monkswood, Arthur joined the Royal Flying Corps on 18th January 1918 having previously served in the South Wales Borderers. He listed his next of kin as his wife Eliza of Bush Terrace, Pantygasseg.

Arthur served with 19 and 157 Squadrons as a Driver until his discharge on 14th December 1918. He was still living with his family in Pantygasseg in 1939 and working as a Coal Haulier. Nothing more is known of his life.

Brown, Lewis. Private, 1916. 2nd Battalion Monmouthshire Regiment

Croes-y-pant
1914 Star, British War Medal, Victory Medal

Born in 1892 Lewis was the son of Samuel and Margaret Brown. Listed on the 1901 census living at Trevethin, by 1911 the family were residing at Croes-y-pant, Mamhilad and Lewis was employed as a Collier. He was also a pre-war Territorial soldier with the 2nd Battalion Monmouthshire Regiment. Lewis is mentioned in the following article printed in the Cambria Daily Leader on 19th March 1914:

WELSH PIT EXPLOSION. CHARGE SAID TO HAVE EXPLODED PREMATURELY.
Owing to the explosion of a firing charge in the Glyntillery Colliery, between Pontypool and Crumlin, Monmouth, yesterday, two men were killed and two seriously injured. The names of the victims are William John Fisher, married, Penyrheol, killed. Ernest Bradford, 19, Penyrheol, killed. Lewis Brown, Mamhilad, severe cuts. Frederick Livell, Pontypool, shock and fracture of the skull. The colliery has only recently been developed after having been closed for many years. Yesterday a gang of men were firing a charge in hard ground when, it is alleged, through some un- explained cause the charge exploded prematurely. Fisher and Bradford were killed instantly. Fisher was decapitated.

Lewis was mobilised with his Battalion on 5th August 1914, arriving in France on 7th November 1914. Surviving the war, he returned home and died in the local area in late 1934, at the early age of 43. Lewis' name is recorded amongst the war survivors on the memorial plaque in Saron Baptist Chapel.

Charles, Isaac Jenkins. Private, 33701. Border Regiment

Parc-y-brain Lane, Penperlleni
British War Medal, Victory Medal

Born in the local area on 10th December 1888 Isaac was baptised at St Peter's church on 13th January 1889. He is listed on the 1891 census living at Beech Cottage, near Saron Baptist Chapel. By 1901 Isaac was living on Parc-y-brain Lane and attending Goytre school, the register recording his father William as a farmer. By 1911 Isaac had left Goytre and was working as a Chemist's Assistant in Cardiff and was lodging in Cathays.

Isaac joined the Army on 26th January 1916, serving overseas with the 1st Battalion, Border Regiment. Surviving the war he was discharged due to wounds or sickness on 10th January 1919. His name is recorded on the Saron Baptist Chapel war memorial.

Returning to employment in the pharmaceutical trade, by 1939 Isaac was working as a Pharmacist Shopkeeper in Croydon, London and died there in 1947, aged 58.

Charles, William John

Parc-y-brain, Penperlleni

Probably the William John Charles who was born on 3rd January 1885 and then baptised at St Peter's on 1st March the same year. He was the son of William and Elizabeth of Parc-y-Brain. William was still living at Parc-y-Brain in 1911 and working as a Dairyman and Horse Dealer.

It has proved impossible to trace his military service although he is recorded as a survivor on the memorial at St Peter's.

By 1939 William was farming at Coed Howell Farm. He died on 10th December 1962 at Sunnyside, Mamhilad aged 77.

Clark, James. 1349, Lance-Corporal. 2nd Battalion Monmouthshire Regiment

Millbrook Place, Little Mill
1914 Star with Clasp, British War Medal, Victory Medal

Born in Shropshire in 1888 James is listed on the 1911 census living at Millbrook Place and working as a Brick Maker.

James enlisted as a Territorial Soldier in the 2nd Battalion Monmouthshire Regiment in 1912, arriving in France with the Battalion on 7th November 1914. Surviving the war, he returned home but nothing more is known of his life.

Collins, F

Listed as a survivor on the memorial at St Peter's, he cannot be positively identified.

Cornish, Reginald. 1343, Private. 2nd Battalion Monmouthshire Regiment

Capel Ed Cottage, Penperlleni
1914 Star with Clasp, British War Medal, Victory Medal

Reginald was born in Glamorganshire on 8th February 1895. He attended Goytre School between 1899 and 1907 and when first registered was living at Capel Ed Cottage. By 1911 he was living with his family at The Gelli and was working as a Brickyard Labourer.

Enlisting for the 2nd Battalion, Monmouthshire Regiment on 17th May 1912 he attended annual training in 1912 and 1913 before being mobilised on the outbreak of war in August 1914. He served in France from 4th November 1914 until 4th December 1915, when he was evacuated to the UK suffering from impetigo.

Upon recovery Reginald was posted to the 3/2nd Battalion, a Reserve unit. As he had enlisted for the Territorial Force for a period of four years, Reginald's term of engagement expired in 1916, and under the Military Service Act (1916) he was discharged from the Army on 13th March of that year. In many cases, men who were discharged as time expired but who still met the criteria of the Military Service Act were re-enlisted or were later conscripted having returned home. Reginald saw no further service, most likely due to his medical record. He is recorded as a survivor on the memorial at St Peter's.

Obviously anxious to receive his war medals, Reginald wrote to the Army in July 1919 requesting the issue of his 1914 Star and clasp, giving his address as 13, Fowler Street, Wainfelin.

By 1939 Reginald was living at Panteg and working as an Underground Timberman. He died on 18th April 1954 at Pontypool District Hospital and had been living at 13 Green View, New Inn at the time of his death.

Cox, C

Listed as survivor on the memorial at St Peter's, he cannot be positively identified.

Cotterell, Albert H. W. Private, 3153. 2nd Battalion Monmouthshire Regiment

Capel Ed, Penperlleni
British War Medal, Victory Medal

Albert Hartland William Cotterell was born in Upton-upon-Severn on 16th December 1884 and by 1901 was living with his family in Malvern Wells, Worcestershire. In 1907 he married Emily Gillan in Worcester.

On the 1918 Absent Voter's List he is recorded as living at Capel Ed, Goytre and serving overseas with the 2nd Battalion Monmouthshire Regiment.

Albert survived the war and is listed as such on the memorial in St Peter's church.

By 1939 Albert and his wife were living in Lewisham, London where he was working as a Builder's Plasterer. He spent the remainder of his life in London and died in the autumn of 1964, aged 79.

Cowles, John George. Driver, 58718. Royal Field Artillery

Pentovy Place, Little Mill

John was born in the Pontypool area on 20th August 1893 and on the 1911 census he is recorded as Cowman at Glascoed. Having previously spent a brief period as a cleaner at Pontypool Road Station he returned to work on the railways in 1914, as a Packer.

During the war John served as a Driver in the Royal Field Artillery but little is known of his service. On the 1918 Absent Voters List he is recorded as living at Pentovy Place, Little Mill.

Surviving the war John is listed on the 1939 register living in Newport. He died on 11th January 1974, aged 80

Cule, James Aaron. Rifleman, 23/1960. NZEF

Llanwenarth Ultra and New Zealand
British War Medal, Victory Medal

James was born in the Pontypridd area in the autumn of 1889 but by 1901 he was living with his family at Llanwenarth Ultra. Sometime between 1901 and the start of the war he emigrated to New Zealand.

He enlisted for the New Zealand Army and embarked for overseas service on 4th March 1916 with the 3rd Battalion New Zealand Rifle Brigade.

James was killed in action on 15th September 1916, aged 27 and is buried in the Serre Road No2 Cemetery at the Somme, France. He is also remembered on the Saron Baptist Chapel memorial.

Cuthbertson, Edward B. Brigadier-General

Goytre Hall
Order of St Michael and St George, CMG, Royal Victorian Order, OBE, Queen's South Africa Medal, King's South Africa Medal, 1914 Star with Clasp, British War Medal, Victory Medal with oakleaf emblem, 1911 Coronation Medal, 1937 Coronation Medal and numerous foreign decorations

Edward Boustead Cuthbertson was born on 13 June 1880 and educated at Marlborough School. He was commissioned into the Argyll & Sutherland Highlanders on 18 October 1899 and promoted Lieutenant on 3 July 1901. During the Boer War he saw action in the advance on Kimberley, the battle of Magersfontein, on operations in Orange Free State, at Paardeberg and Driefontein and at Zilikats Nek.

He was placed on Half Pay in February 1904 and on Retired Pay in January 1908. During the period 1908-1914 he served as Equerry to Princess Beatrice and was awarded the M.V.O. 4th Class. His service to Princess Beatrice, wife of Prince Henry of Battenberg and mother of Queen Victoria Eugenie of Spain also resulted in the award of several more foreign orders. During this time he also held the rank of Major in the Isle of Wight Rifles, Prince Henry being Captain and Governor of the island.

Edward later joined the Monmouthshire Regiment and was Lieutenant-Colonel and Commanding Officer of 2nd Battalion during the period 1911-1915. With the outbreak of war he sailed with his battalion on the Manchester Importer to Le Havre on 5 November 1914. He was wounded at Ypres in May 1915 and invalided home. Letters sent home by 2nd Battalion soldiers describe how during the fierce fighting at Ypres Cuthbertson fought with a rifle and bayonet, just like a Private soldier. Surviving the war and having been awarded numerous decorations, Cuthbertson returned home and is included on the list of survivors on the St Peter's Church memorial.

He was promoted Brigadier-General in 1916 and retired from the Army in 1922. For his wartime services he was awarded the C.M.G. (London Gazette 16 March 1915), was mentioned in dispatches (London Gazette 17 February 1915, 1 January 1916) and was awarded the Russian Order of St. Stanislaus, 3rd Class (London Gazette 25 August 1915).

An active gentleman farmer in the inter-war years, in 1928 he was created the High Sheriff of Surrey. He maintained links with the Territorial Army and was active in the formation of the Hampshire Land Defence Volunteers – the Home Guard, prior to and in the early years of the Second World War. Edward Cuthbertson died on 13 May 1942.

Davis, Jack. Private, 2105. Monmouthshire Regiment / Labour Corps

The Nutshell, Penperlleni
1914/15 Star, British War Medal, Victory Medal

Jack was born in 1892. He enlisted for the Monmouthshire Regiment at Newport on 10th August 1914, giving his address as 1 Woodside, Crumlin. Posted to the 1st Battalion he arrived in France on 13th March 1915.

Jack's service record shows that he was presumed killed in action during the fierce fighting at Frezenberg on 8th May 1915 and notification was sent to his wife at Stow Hill, Newport. It then transpired that another Monmouthshire soldier with the same name had been killed on the same day and Jack's wife had to write a great many letters to the war office explaining that she was still receiving weekly letters from her husband and that he was very much still alive.

Jack was later transferred to the Labour Corps but his previous good luck ran out on 6th April 1918 when he was shot in the head. Surviving the injury, he was evacuated back to the UK where he recovered enough to re-join his unit only to proceed again to France on 29th November 1918, a fortnight after the war ended.

On the 1918 Absent Voters List, Jack's address is given as The Nutshell, Goytre and it was to that address he went to on his eventual discharge in March 1919. Nothing more is known of his life.

Davies, Edward John. Private, 7480, 1st Battalion King's Shropshire Light Infantry

California, links with Nantyderry
1914 Star, British War Medal, Victory Medal

Edward was born in California in 1876. On the 1891 census he is listed as living in Grosmont with his Grandfather, Uncle and siblings. Either serving at the outbreak of war or a recalled reservist, Edward arrived in France on 10th September 1914. He was killed in action just over a month later on 25th October, aged 38. His body was not recovered and he is remembered on the Ploegsteert memorial,

Belgium. Edward was the sister of Martha Jane Lloyd of Nantyderry and is also commemorated on the memorial in St Peter's church.

Day, F.C.

Listed as survivor on the memorial at St Peter's church he cannot be positively identified.

Day, Thomas. 3rd Battalion South Wales Borderers

Park View, Penperlleni

On the 1918 Absent Voters List, Thomas' address is given as Park View, Goytre and that he was serving with the 3rd Battalion, South Wales Borderers. He is also commemorated as a survivor on the plaque at St Peter's church. Nothing more is known about him.

Dobbs, George. Private, 21419, 10th Battalion South Wales Borderers

Llwyncelyn Farm (near Goytre Wharf)
1914/15 Star, British War Medal, Victory Medal

George Dobbs was baptised at St Peter's church on 5th February 1893. At the time of the 1891 census the Dobbs family was living at No.2 Capel Ed where George's father Richard was employed as a labourer. By 1901 the family had moved to Yew Tree Cottage and by 1911 they were farming at Llwyncelyn Farm, near Goytre Wharf.

At the outbreak of war George enlisted at Newport for the 10th (1st Gwent) Battalion, South Wales Borderers and arrived in France with them on 3rd December 1915.

The Welsh Division saw its first major action during the Somme Offensive when they were tasked with capturing Mametz Wood. The first assault was made on 7th July 1916 by the 16th Welsh and 11th South Wales Borderers, resulting in heavy casualties for both Battalions and the attack faltering. At 10.00hrs the 10th South Wales Borderers were ordered into the assault but did not arrive at the area until noon with their Commanding Officer being killed whilst bringing them forward.

The attack was called off later that day and plans to assault again on the 8th and 9th July were formed, then cancelled.

The second assault was made on 10th July by Battalions of the Welsh Regiment and Royal Welsh Fusiliers who achieved a foothold in the wood. The 15th Welsh were then sent up in support and good progress was made. In the afternoon two further Battalions, including the 10th South Wales Borderers, were also sent in support and reached the northern end of the wood. By the end of the day the German forces were forced to withdraw. The plan for 11th July was to complete the capture of the wood and after fierce fighting the Germans completely withdrew that night.

After the fighting at Mametz the 10th South Wales Borderers returned to the Reserve and the following week were at Courcelles-Au-Bois where they took over front line trenches on 18th July. The Battalion came out of the line again on 22nd July but returned to the trenches again on 26th July to relieve the 11th South Wales Borderers. The Battalion war diary for 26th July reads:

Battalion in TRENCHES. Quiet day, 1 Killed, 10/21419 Pte Dobbs, G

George was buried in the Sucrerie Military Cemetery, France and is also commemorated on the St Peter's church war memorial. His younger brother John Arthur Dobbs was killed in 1918.

The capture of Mametz Wood cost the 38th (Welsh) Division nearly 4,000 casualties, a fifth of its fighting force and it was not used again in an attack until the summer of 1917. A Welsh Dragon memorial (left) was erected there in 1986 by the Western Front Association and was restored in 2016.

Dobbs, John Arthur. Private, 154127, Machine Gun Corps

Llwyncelyn Farm (near Goytre Wharf)
British War Medal, Victory Medal

John Arthur Dobbs, the younger brother of George Dobbs, was baptised at St Peter's church on 13th August 1899. He grew up with his brother at Llwyncelyn Farm and became a farm labourer.

John served initially with the Loyal North Lancashire Regiment before being transferred to the Machine Gun Corps, which had been formed in 1915.

John died on 6th July 1918, of wounds suffered in an accident, two years to the month since his brother had fallen. Aged 18 when he was killed, John is buried at the Bagneux cemetery on the Somme and is also commemorated on the war memorial at St Peter's church.

Edmunds, Daniel. Private, 39572, Labour Corps

Rose Tree Cottage, Goytre

Little information can be found about Daniel. The 1918 Absent Voters List records him living at Rose Tree Cottage, Goytre and serving with the Agricultural Company of the Labour Corps. His name is also recorded on the memorial in St Peter's church, listing him as a survivor.

Edwards, Albert. Private, T4/274871, Army Service Corps

Ty-twmpyn, Penperlleni
British War Medal, Victory Medal

Albert served with the Packers and Loaders of the Army Service Corps. Surviving the war he is commemorated as a survivor on the memorial at St Peter's church. On the 1918 Absent Voters List his address is recorded as Ty-twmpyn.

Emery, Thomas. Acting Corporal, 78039, Royal Army Medical Corps

Brook Cottage, Penperlleni
British War Medal, Victory Medal

Born in 1886, Thomas enlisted in November 1915 at Newport, joining the Royal Army Medical Corps. Prior to joining the Army he had been living in Risca and working as a School Teacher. Promoted quickly through the ranks he was an Acting Sergeant by May 1916.

Thomas saw service overseas with No.84 Casualty Clearing Station, survived the war and was discharged from the Army in September 1919. On the 1918 Absent Voters List his address is recorded as Brook Cottage, Goytre.

Continuing his teaching career, by 1939 he was living in Abercarn and employed as a Head Teacher. Thomas died in Upton-upon-Severn in late 1946, aged 60.

Evans MC, Arthur E. Lieutenant, Royal Field Artillery

Ty Perllan, Penperlleni
Military Cross, 1914/15 Star, British War Medal, Victory Medal

Arthur Edward Evans was born on 12th February 1889. He was the son of Edwin and Sarah Evans and at the time of the 1891 census was living at The Old Stores, where his father was employed as a Wheelwright.

On the outbreak of war, Arthur enlisted in the Royal Field Artillery and arrived in France on 21st July 1915. He progressed through the ranks to Sergeant before being commissioned as a 2nd Lieutenant. Arthur survived the war and on 10th January 1919 it was announced in the London Gazette that he had been awarded the Military Cross.

2nd Lt, Arthur Edward Evans, RFA

(Spec Res), attd C/150th Bde

When two guns of his battery had been put out of action and the camouflage set on fire by heavy shelling, and the ammunition in the gun pits was exploding, he and four NCOs dragged the remainder of the guns down a slope away from the fire.

Shortly afterwards he was again called to come into action in support of infantry, which he did most effectively until he was severely wounded. He displayed great gallantry and remarkable presence of mind in difficult circumstances.

On the 1918 Absent Voters List Arthur is recorded as living at Ty Perllan, which is understood to be one the buildings that is now part of the Goytre Arms public house. He is recorded as a survivor on the memorial plaque at Saron Baptist Chapel.

Post war Arthur joined Cardiff Police and rose to the rank of Sergeant before retiring in 1942. He died in South Glamorgan in 1977, aged 88.

Evans, Benjamin. Guardsman, 1348, 1ˢᵗ Battalion Welsh Guards

Byrgwm Mawr, Upper Llanover
1914/15 Star, British War Medal, Victory Medal

Born in Llangunnor, Carmarthenshire in 1890, Benjamin is recorded on the 1901 census living with his family who were farming at Llanellen. By the start of the Great War they had moved to Byrgwm Mawr and Benjamin was employed at Llanover Estate.

The Welsh Guards were formed on 26ᵗʰ February 1915 and Benjamin was an early recruit. Arriving in France on 17ᵗʰ August 1915 the 1ˢᵗ Battalion first saw action on 27ᵗʰ September 1915, the opening day of the Battle of Loos. 54 soldiers of the Battalion were killed on that date including Benjamin. Aged 25 at the time of his death, Benjamin's body was not recovered and he is remembered on the Loos Memorial and on the memorial at Abergavenny Market Hall.

Evans, E

E Evans is recorded as a casualty on the memorial in St Peter's church. Unfortunately, due to his common name it has been so far impossible to trace him.

Evans, G

Listed as survivor on the memorial at St Peter's, he cannot be positively identified in records.

Evans, James Thomas. Driver, 108185, Royal Engineers

Llanover School House
1914/15 Star, British War Medal, Victory Medal

James was born in 1882 and on the 1891 census he is recorded living at Llanover School House where his father was a Gardener. By 1911 he was employed as a Groom at Llanover House.

Enlisting on 28th May 1915 James arrived in France on 3rd December of that year with 124 Field Company, Royal Engineers. Apart from 10 days leave to the UK in January 1917, he served in France until he was discharged in March 1919.

On the 1918 Absent Voters List his address is given as Pen-yr-heol, Upper Llanover and upon discharge from the Army he lived in Clifton Road, Abergavenny. Nothing more is known of his life.

Evans, W

Listed as survivor on the memorial at St Peter's, he cannot be positively identified in records.

Goodwin, William. Private, 266503, 14th Battalion South Lancashire Regiment

Woodside View, Little Mill

Born in Worcestershire in 1885, by 1911 William was living at Woodside View, Little Mill and working as a Labourer at the nearby brickworks. Serving with the 14th Battalion of the South Lancashire Regiment he survived the war. William died in Worcestershire in 1939, aged 53.

Griffiths, T. Royal Field Artillery

T Griffiths is recorded as a survivor on the Saron Baptist Chapel Memorial. Unfortunately, due to his common name it has been impossible to trace him.

Griffiths, William John. 3509 Lance Corporal, 1st Battalion South Wales Borderers

Croes yn y pant, Mamhilad
British War Medal

Born in 1897, William is recorded on the 1911 census as a 14 year old Assistant Milkman living with his family at Croes yn y pant (now known as Croes y pant), Mamhilad.

Serving with the 1/1st (Brecknockshire) Battalion of the South Wales Borderers, a Territorial Force unit, he most likely spent the majority of his overseas service in India. His single medal entitlement of the British War Medal shows that he did not serve in an operational theatre at any point. He is possibly the W Griffiths who is recorded as a survivor on the Saron Baptist Chapel Memorial.

Guest, Henry. Private, 1345, 2nd Battalion Monmouthshire Regiment

Myrtle Cottage, School Lane, Penperlleni
1914 Star, British War Medal, Victory Medal

Born in 1895, on the 1911 census Henry is listed as boarding at Myrtle Cottage, School Lane, Goytre and employed as a Carpenter. A pre-war Territorial soldier with the 2nd Battalion Monmouthshire Regiment he arrived in France with the Battalion on 7th November 1914.

On 10th December 1914 the 2nd Battalion began their second four day period in the front-line trenches. The following day Henry became the 10th casualty of the war for the Battalion, most likely killed by a sniper. He was buried in Calvaire Military Cemetery and is also remembered on the war memorial in St Peter's church.

Henry's medals were sent to his next of kin but they were not received. They were subsequently returned to the issuing authority who disposed of them in 1920.

Guppy, John Henry. Private, 54014, Welsh Regiment, Labour Corps & Royal Defence Corps

Royal Oak Cottages, Monkswood
British War Medal, Victory Medal

Born on 4th April 1897, John enlisted for the Army on 26th September 1917. He gave his address as Royal Oak Cottages, Monkswood and trade as Colliery Labourer.

John was in trouble several times during his service. On 5th February 1918 he overstayed his leave pass by four hours and was punished with three days confined to barracks. On 30th March 1918 he was again missing from camp, this time for three hours and was punished with another three days confined to barracks. Finally, on 4th September 1918 he was negligent whilst on escort duty and received the same punishment as before.

Transferred from the Welsh Regiment to the Labour Corps he transferred again in June 1918 to the Royal Defence Corps, a home defence unit. Discharged in 1919 John did see some service in France during his time in the Army, as shown by his award of the British War Medal and Victory Medal.

In 1939 John was living at Cefn Bungalow, Monkswood and employed as a General Labourer. He died in Newport on 7th February 1984, aged 86.

Gwatkin, Gilbert. Private, 290800, Labour Corps

Church Farm, Nantyderry

Gilbert was born on 17th June 1896 and baptised at St Peter's church on 20th July. On the 1911 census he is recorded as a Farmer's son at Church Farm. Serving with the Agricultural Company of the Labour Corps there is no evidence that he was posted overseas at any point. His name is recorded amongst the survivors on the memorial plaque in St Peter's church.

In 1939 Gilbert was employed as a Horseman and Shepherd in the Cardiff rural district. He died on 8th September 1965, aged 69 and at the time of his death had been living at The Narth, Monmouth.

Harding, Richard. Private, 1701814, Labour Corps

Gardener's Cottage, Nantyderry
British War Medal, Victory Medal

Richard was born on 29th September 1882 and was the elder brother of Samuel Edward Harding. By 1911 he was living at Gardener's Cottage, Nantyderry and working as a Groom.

Richard joined the Army on 27th November 1915 under the Derby Scheme, which returned men to their civilian life until their age and marital status group was called forward for service. Richard was duly mobilised on 27th March 1916 and after very brief spells in the Welsh Regiment and Liverpool Regiment he was posted to the Labour Corps, serving with them in France with an Agricultural Company. On 30th September 1917 he was fined for losing his steel helmet.

Surviving the war, Richard was discharged in September 1919 and returned to Goytre. His name is recorded as a survivor on the memorial at St Peter's church. In 1939 Richard was still living at Gardener's Cottage. He died in the Chepstow area in 1962, aged 80.

Harding, Samuel Edward

Gardener's Cottage, Nantyderry

Samuel Edward Harding was baptised at St Peter's church on 25th March 1894, the son of John and Elizabeth Harding of Gardener's Cottage and younger brother of Richard Harding. By 1911 he was working as a Draper's Assistant and living at Lion House, Pontypool.

Nothing is known of his wartime service apart from that he is recorded as a survivor on the memorial in St Peter's.

Richard is listed on the Ellis Island immigration records as arriving in New York aboard the SS Orduna on 29th June 1919, intending to settle in Ohio and giving his trade as Boilermaker. Nothing more is known of his life.

Hardwick, J. Royal Field Artillery

J Hardwick is recorded as a survivor on the Saron Baptist Chapel Memorial. Unfortunately, it has been impossible to trace him.

Harper, Evi. Private, 22002, South Wales Borderers & Labour Corps

Twyn Cecil Cottage, Monkswood
1914/15 Star, British War Medal, Victory Medal

Born in 1889 and living at Twyn Cecil Cottage, Monkswood, Evi enlisted for the South Wales Borderers, arriving in France with the 11th Battalion on 3rd December 1915. Later serving with the Labour Corps he survived the war.

Evi died in 1920 at the early age of 31. He is probably the E Harper recorded on the list of dead on the memorial plaque at St Peter's church, having died as a result of his service.

Harry, David. Lance Corporal, 17342, 5ᵗʰ Battalion King's Shropshire Light Infantry

Elm Tree Cottage, Pencroesoped
1914/15 Star, British War Medal, Victory Medal

David Harry was born in Bettws Newydd in 1889. By 1911 he was a Gamekeeper and living at Elm Tree Cottage, Pencroesoped.

Serving with the 5ᵗʰ Battalion, King's Shropshire Light Infantry he arrived in France on 23ʳᵈ June 1915. David was killed in action on 30ᵗʰ August 1916 and is commemorated on the Thiepval memorial and at Saron Baptist Chapel.

Harry, William. Sergeant, 10029, Gordon Highlanders

1914 Star, British War Medal, Victory Medal

Listed as a survivor on the Saron Baptist Chapel memorial, William was either a regular soldier or pre-war reservist who arrived in France on 13ᵗʰ August 1914, just nine days after the war started. He was later captured and became a prisoner of war but survived. Nothing more is known of his service or life.

Higgs, Albert Edward. Lance Corporal, 3164. 2ⁿᵈ Battalion Monmouthshire Regiment

Rose Tree Cottage, Mamhilad
British War Medal, Victory Medal

Albert Higgs was born in Glamorgan on 23ʳᵈ August 1896. By 1911 he was living at Rose Cottage, Mamhilad and was working as a Plasterer's Labourer.

Serving with the 2ⁿᵈ Battalion, Monmouthshire Regiment, Albert arrived in France on 27ᵗʰ October 1917. Surviving the war he returned to Monmouthshire and is listed on the Saron Baptist Chapel memorial.

Albert married in 1918 and by 1939 was living in Pontypool and working as a Builder's Labourer. He died on 10ᵗʰ November 1965, aged 69 and had been living in Penygarn at the time of his death.

Higgs, William Thomas. Private, 1344. 2nd Battalion Monmouthshire Regiment

Glebe Cottage, Mamhilad
1914 Star, British War Medal, Victory Medal

William Higgs was born in Merthyr on 1st June 1894. On the 1901 census he is recorded living at Glebe Cottage, Mamhilad. By 1909, aged 14 he was working as a cleaner at Pontypool Road Station. A pre-war Territorial soldier with the 2nd Battalion Monmouthshire Regiment he arrived in France on 7th November 1914.

William was killed in action on 1st July 1916, the first day of the Battle of The Somme, where the Battalion was supporting the attacking infantry. Commemorated on the Thiepval memorial he is also remembered on the Saron Baptist Chapel memorial.

Humphreys, Ernest C. Second Lieutenant, Canadian Forces

Pen-y-stair, Mamhilad

Born on 22nd March 1903 in Mamhilad, Ernest attended Goytre School between 1895 and 1905. He is listed on the 1911 census as living at Pen-y-stair and working as a Rural Postman.

Emigrating to Canada he served with Canadian Forces during the war. Ernest is listed as a survivor on the memorial at Saron Baptist Chapel. Nothing more is known of his life.

James, John. Gunner, 214703, Royal Field Artillery

Millbrook Place, Little Mill
British War Medal

Not traceable on censuses John served with the Royal Field Artillery, arriving overseas sometime after the start of 1916. His medal index card shows that he was only entitled to the British War Medal, indicating that he most likely spent the war on garrison duty in a non-operational area such as India. On the 1918 Absent Voters List he is recorded living at 2 Millbrook Place, Little Mill.

James, John David. Private, 3910, Monmouthshire & Welsh Regiments

Pencroesoped Farm

John was born in Aberystwyth on 10th February 1887. In the 1911 census he is recorded as a Farmer's Son, living and working at Pencroesoped Farm, Goytre. Initially serving in the Monmouthshire Regiment, James was transferred to the 1/6 Welsh Regiment which was deployed as a Pioneer Battalion in France. He survived the war and returned to Goytre. By 1939 John was living and working at Yew Tree Farm, Goytre and died in 1961, aged 73.

Jenkins, Arthur. Private, 46948, 1st Battalion Welsh Regiment

Pentovy Place, Little Mill
British War Medal, Victory Medal

Born in 1888, Arthur served overseas with the 1st Battalion, Welsh Regiment sometime after the start of 1916. On the 1918 Absent Voters List he is recorded living at 2 Pentovy Place, Little Mill. He was discharged on 1st April 1919 with an address of The Butcher's Arms, Frogmore Street, Abergavenny.

Jenkins, Iltyd Charles. Corporal, WR/22221, Royal Engineers

New Barn Farm, Penperlleni
British War Medal, Victory Medal

Iltyd was born on 11th September 1897 and baptised at St Peter's church on 10th October the same year. By 1911 he was a schoolboy, living at New Barn Farm, Goytre.

He was called up for Army service in January 1917 and was in France just over a month later, serving as a Pioneer with a Railway Company. His rapid deployment to France is probably due to his civilian role as a surveyor. Iltyd survived the war remaining in the Army until 1920, by which time he had been promoted to Corporal and re-traded as a Clerk.

Upon discharge he returned to Goytre and is listed as a survivor on the memorial in St Peter's church. Iltyd died on 15th April 1991 in Farnborough, aged 93, possibly the last Goytre veteran of the Great War.

Jenkins, Edward Arthur. Private, M2/152023, Army Service Corps

Arrow Cottage, Penperlleni

Born in Usk in 1880, by 1911 Edward was employed as a Carpenter and living in Arrow Cottage, Penperlleni. During the war he served with a Tractor Company of the Army Service Corps. It is not known if he served overseas.

Surviving the war his name is listed as a survivor on the memorial in St Peter's church. Edward died in the local area in 1963, aged 83.

Jenkins, Phillip. Private, 15257, South Wales Borderers & Royal Welsh Fusiliers

Ty-llwydd, Pencroesoped
1914/15 Star, British War Medal, Victory Medal

Phillip was baptised at St Peter's church on 8th March 1885. On the 1901 census he is listed as living at Ty-llwydd, where his father was a woodcutter.

Initially serving with the 1st Battalion South Wales Borderers, Phillip arrived in France on 26th January 1915 and was later transferred to the 1st Battalion, Royal Welsh Fusiliers.

Phillip survived the war and his name is recorded on the list of survivors on the memorial plaque at St Peter's church. Nothing more is known of his life.

Jenkins, William John. 260095 Royal Engineers

Ty Coch, Penperlleni

William was baptised at St Peter's church on 7th June 1891. By 1911 he was living at Ty Coch, Penperlleni and employed as a Mechanic. During the war he served with the Royal Engineers and his name is recorded on the list of survivors on the memorial plaque at St Peter's church. Nothing more is known of his life.

Jones, Edwin James. Private, 46825, 1st Battalion South Wales Borderers

Mill Cottage, Pantglas, Upper Llanover
British War Medal, Victory Medal

Born in 1899, Edwin is listed on the 1911 census as a schoolboy living at Mill Cottage, Pantglas, where his father was a wheelwright.

Serving with the 1st Battalion South Wales Borderers, Edwin was also deployed with the 170th Tunnelling Company, working to dig tunnels on the Western Front to disrupt enemy activity through listening posts and exploding mines.

Edwin survived the war and returned home. Nothing more is known of his life. He was the brother of William Jones.

Jones, Evan. Master Mariner

New Barn Farm, Mamhilad
British War Medal, Mercantile Marine War Medal

Born in Dyffryn, Merionethshire on 11th January 1879, Evan qualified as a 2nd Mate in 1899. Serving as master and Captain of merchant vessels during the war, the 1918 Absent Voters List gives his address as New Barn Farm, Goytre.

Evan survived the war and by 1939 was living at The Haven, Nantyderry (just up the lane from St Peter's church). Nothing more is known of his life.

Jones, G. Private, 2nd Battalion Monmouthshire Regiment

Listed as a survivor on the memorial in the Saron Baptist Chapel it has been impossible to discover anything about him.

Jones, Ivor David. Able Seaman, Z/2839, Royal Navy

Cider Mill, Saron Road, Penperlleni,

British War Medal, Victory Medal

Ivor was born on 11th June 1897 and baptised on 31st October at Llanover. He is recorded on the 1911 census as living at Cider Mill, Goytre.

Enlisting for the Royal Naval Reserve on 10th January 1916, Ivor served on shore bases before being posted to H.M.S. Malaya, a battleship armed with eight 15 inch guns and fourteen 6 inch guns. Ivor joined the crew of Malaya on 8th June 1916, probably as a casualty replacement as it was less than a fortnight since she had been hit eight times at the Battle of Jutland and had 65 men killed.

Ivor served on Malaya until 1919, when he was discharged. On the 1918 Absent Voters List he is recorded as living at Moss Rose Cottage. He is also recorded as a survivor on the memorial plaque at Saron Baptist Chapel. In 1939 Ivor was living at Lapstone Cottage (next to canal bridge number 76) and working as a Labourer. He died in early 1971, aged 73.

Jones, Vernon. Private, 9726, 2/4th Battalion Yorkshire Regiment

Ty Llwydd, Upper Llanover
British War Medal, Victory Medal

Born in the local area in 1895, by 1911 Vernon was a 16 year old Woodsman living at Ty Llwydd. Vernon joined the Army on 18th September 1916 and was posted to the 2/4th Battalion, Yorkshire Regiment. He served in France from 10th January 1917 to 23rd May 1917, when he was invalided to hospital in Liverpool. Upon recovering Vernon returned to France for a second time, from 8th September 1917 to 22nd November 1917. He was discharged from the Army on 6th June 1918 as no longer medically fit for service. Nothing more is known of his life.

Jones, William. Private, 5818, Royal Army Medical Corps

Mill Cottage, Pantglas, Upper Llanover
1914 Star, British War Medal, Victory Medal

Brother of Edwin Jones of Pantglas Mill, William was likely either a pre-war regular soldier or reservist. He served in France from early October 1914 with the 14th General Hospital and survived the war. Nothing more is known about his life.

Jones, William Robert. Private, 48225, Welsh Regiment

Brook Cottage, Little Mill
British War Medal, Victory Medal

Not traceable due to his common name, Arthur served overseas with the Welsh Regiment sometime after the start of 1916. He is listed on the 1918 Absent Voters List as living at 1 Brook Cottage, Little Mill.

Kirby, Sidney Henry. 2nd Lieutenant, Border Regiment

1914/15 Star, British War Medal, Victory Medal

Sidney was born in London in 1891. He was the grandson of Colonel Henry Byrde of Goytre House by his daughter, Frances Byrde Kirby (1861-1896) and attended Goytre School between 1895 and 1897.

Serving as a Platoon Commander attached to C Company of the 1/5 Highland Light Infantry, Sidney was killed in action at Gallipoli on 19th December 1915, whilst leading an assault against enemy positions. He is remembered on both the war memorial in St Peter's and on a separate plaque in the church dedicated to him.

Knight, Charles Ernest Vickery. Private, 41349, 2nd Battalion South Wales Borderers

Mill Street, Usk
British War Medal, Victory Medal

Charles was born in Usk and baptised there on Christmas Eve 1898. On the 1911 census he is recorded as a schoolboy living on Mill Street, where his father worked as a wood turner.

Enlisting at Usk for the South Wales Borderers, Charles was serving with the 2nd Battalion when he was killed in action on 10th March 1918, aged 19 years.

Charles is buried in the Poelcapelle British Cemetery in Belgium and is also commemorated on the war memorial in St Peter's church and on the Usk town memorial.

Lewis, Percy Thomas. Lance Corporal, 31083, 10th Battalion South Wales Borderers

Ty'r Ewen, Penperlleni
British War Medal, Victory Medal

Percy Thomas Lewis was born in Goytre on 2nd July 1896 to William and Annie Lewis. By 1901 Annie had died and the family were living at Hendre Isaf, Llanover, the home of Percy's Grandfather, John. By 1911 Percy's father had remarried, to Margaret Lewis and the family were living at Ty'r - Ewen, Penperlleni, off Star Road.

Percy enlisted in Cardiff for the 10th Battalion, South Wales Borderers and was posted to France sometime after the start of 1916. By 2nd July 1918, his 22nd birthday, Percy had been appointed to the rank of Lance Corporal. The Battalion war diary for that day reads:

A tragedy occurred at the HQ at LEALUILLERS early in the morning of the 2nd July. The HQ was shelled and direct hits were observed on the house where the HQ was located – with the result of 2 officers and 8 OR killed and 2 officers and 8 OR wounded.

Percy was one of the 8 OR (Other Ranks) killed. A comprehensive obituary was published in the Abergavenny Chronicle exactly a month after his death.

GOYTRE. DEATH on Active Service. With deep regret we have to chronicle the death in action in France, on July 2nd, of Lce.-Cpl. Percy Thomas Lewis, S.W.B., the youngest son of, W. Lewis, Tyr-y-wen Goytrey. In a letter bearing the sad news of his death it was stated that a shell struck the building in which he was at the time, killing him instantly. A pathetic feature of this young soldier's death was that it happened on his birthday.

He was born at the Lower Hendre, Llanover, on July 2nd, 1896, received his elementary education at Llanover School, and later on entered the West Mon. Intermediate School, where he gave every satisfaction to the masters as a scholar who applied himself diligently to all his studies.

By further private study he passed his examinations for the Excise, in the office of which he served for some time at Cardiff, then at Pontypool. From here he was called to the colours, joining the South Wales Borderers and in due time went over with them to France. From there he wrote many letters to his friends, in all of which he expressed his delight at receiving heartening letters from home, and showed his true estimate of the nature and merits of the world-wide conflict in which he took part.

In the year 1905, when the Revival was in its strength, at the tender age of nine he was one of one 30 new members who were received into the Congregational Church. At Hanover. From that day onwards he continued to manifest the deepest interest that concerned the welfare of the Church and. The Sunday-school. Thus, death has removed from our midst, at the early age of 22, an engaging personality that had I already given sure signs of forcefulness of character and high promise of a successful career in life. Those with whom he served in the regiment of the S. W.B. all bear united testimony to his excellent soldierly qualities, and particularly to his sterling Christian character. It is no exaggeration, it is only bare truth, to say that our young friend, like many more high and low has given his life for his country and for the world, and, let us firmly hope, not in vain. Such heroic deaths, endured on the world's battlefields, are, alas and perforce, the costly price of the world's advancement. It is this thought which now, as in time to come, will most surely bring real and solid comfort to every, stricken and perplexed heart that has been called to" sorrow in this great Armageddon of the nations.

Percy was buried in the Varennes British Cemetery and is not believed to be commemorated in the Goytre area.

Lloyd, Edward 214725, Gunner, Royal Field Artillery

Pen-yr-heol, Mamhilad
British War Medal, Victory Medal

Edward Arthur Lloyd was born locally in 1878 and by 1911 was living with his parents at Penyrheol, Goytre and working as a mason's labourer.

Serving as a Gunner in the Royal Field Artillery he survived the war and is recorded as a survivor on the memorial at St Peter's church. On the 1918 Absent Voters List he is recorded as living at Yew Tree Cottage.

Edward died in the Abergavenny area in 1957, aged 78.

46

Lloyd, Jonah Henry. Private, 27761, 18th Battalion Welsh Regiment

Croes y pant

Jonah was born in Shropshire in 1881. At the time of the 1911 census he was living at Croes y pant, Mamhilad and working as a Collier. He enlisted for the Army at Bridgnorth, Shropshire on 12th February 1915 but only served until 15th April 1915, being discharged as no longer being required.

Merrick, Charles William. Staff Sergeant, M2/281372, Army Service Corps

Feltham Cottage, Penperlleni

Charles William Merrick was born on 29th September 1889 and was baptised in Mamhilad on 5th November of that year. His father, also named Charles, was a School Master at the Reformatory School in Little Mill, which is where the family is recorded as living on the 1901 census. Charles's father died in September 1906, from injuries received six months previously when he was struck by a motor car near Little Mill Railway Bridge.

By 1911 Charles was employed as a Mechanical Engineer and was living with his widowed mother at Feltham Cottage, Newtown Road, Penperlleni.

On 11th December 1915 Charles enlisted at Abergavenny for the Army Service Corps (Mechanical Transport). He gave his occupation as Agricultural Engineer and next of kin as his mother Martha, of Feltham Cottage.

Charles was not actually mobilised until the 1st January 1917, which means he had probably enlisted under the Derby Scheme, which enabled a man to join the Army but then return home until his age and status group (marital and employment type) were called up.

On mobilisation Charles was immediately promoted to Acting Sergeant, most likely due to his experience as a Mechanical Engineer. Serving in Fulham and later Worcester, Charles saw out the war in the UK and was promoted to Acting Staff Sergeant. He had received papers to proceed to France when the war ended. Due to his expertise, Charles was retained by the Army until he could be replaced and finally left the Army on 19th February 1920.

Following his discharge Charles returned to Goytre where he married Dorothy and had two children. Charles had met his future wife during the war when she was serving with the Women's Forage Corps. Based only in the UK, members of this 6,000 strong unit were deployed as hay balers, sack makers and menders, sheet repairers, thatchers, chaffing hands, drivers and clerks. Their roles enabled more men to be released from their civilian jobs for military service.

Charles was later one of two Goytre enumerators for the 1939 Register, going house to house recording details of each occupant, although apparently some were very reluctant to give their details!

Charles was a gifted pianist and is listed as a Music Teacher on the 1939 register; he was also the organist at St Peter's Church for many years. Charles died on 9th June 1960, aged 70.

Morgan, Alfred. Private, 91476, King's Liverpool Regiment & Royal Army Medical Corps

Ivy Cottage, Little Mill
British War Medal, Victory Medal

Alfred Morgan was born in Little Mill in 1899. On 4th September 1917 and now a Farm Labourer, Alfred enlisted at Pontypool. Serving with the 4th Battalion, King's Liverpool Regiment he arrived in France on 20th April 1918 and was wounded on 24th September the same year. His injury did not require evacuation to the UK and Alfred remained in France until 17th December 1918. In May 1919 he was transferred to the Royal Army Medical Corps and left the Army on 19th August of that year.

Morgan, Azariah Decimus. Private, 3452034, United States Army

Cloud County, Kansas, United States

Born in Hollis, Cloud County, Kansas in 1892, Azariah was named after his father[1], a farmer who had emigrated from Goytre with his brother, William in the early 1880s to seek new opportunities. Azariah was the brother of Ulysses Grant Morgan and a cousin of William Morgan of Pwllmeyric and Lewis Earl Morgan, also of Kansas. He enlisted in the US Army in 1918 and was honourably discharged on 13th June 1919. Azariah died in 1975.

This photograph of Azariah (front right) and his sons includes Azariah Decimus (rear left) and Ulysses (second from left, front row), who both served with the US Army in the Great War.

Morgan, Benjamin. 2nd Lieutenant, Royal Field Artillery

Bussy View, Mamhilad
British War Medal, Victory Medal

Benjamin was born in Goytre in 1892 and was the brother of Clifford Louis Morgan. On the 1911 census he is recorded living at Yew Tree Cottage, Goytre and employed as a Coal Hewer.

In February 1913 Benjamin enlisted for the Royal Artillery but purchased his discharge on 2nd July 1914, only to re-enlist on 3rd September the same year, soon after the outbreak of war and had his discharge payment refunded.

---

[1] Azariah Morgan; born 1862 in Goytre, died 1937 in Cloud County, Kansas

Benjamin was commissioned as a 2nd Lieutenant on 10th June 1918 and survived the war; his name is recorded as a survivor on the Saron Baptist Chapel memorial. On the 1918 Absent Voters List his address is listed as Bussy View. Benjamin died in Worcestershire on 15th October 1959, aged 67.

Morgan, Clifford Louis. Private, 19977, Army Cycling Corps & Army Service Corps

Bussy View, Mamhilad
British War Medal, Victory Medal

Born on 25th September 1898 and the brother of Benjamin Morgan, Clifford enlisted underage at 16, declaring his age as 19. He was posted to the 2/3rd Battalion, Monmouthshire Regiment, a Reserve unit responsible for training recruits before posting them to the front-line Monmouthshire Battalions.

Clifford was transferred to the Army Cycling Corps and served in France from April 1917. Gassed later that year he was evacuated to the UK in June 1918, diagnosed with a weak heart. On the 1918 Absent Voters List his address is recorded as Bussy View.

In 1920, despite his heart problem, Clifford managed to join the Royal Navy. He served until 1923 before being discharged for headaches, giddiness and chronic sea sickness. His records note that his three years Army service counted towards his Navy good conduct badges.

Clifford returned home and died in the local area in 1966.

Morgan, David Hugh. South Wales Borderers

The Wern, Penperlleni

Born in Goytre on 6th May 1869, David is listed as a Farmer at The Wern on the 1901 census. He was the Uncle of William Morgan and Lewis Earl Morgan.

Despite being aged 45 at the start of the war, he enlisted and served as a Private in the South Wales Borderers. David survived the war and is listed as such on the memorial at Saron Baptist Chapel. He was an active member of the Chapel as well as Chairman of the Parish Council for many years.

In 1939 David was farming at The Gwynedd, Penperlleni and died on 1st February 1946, aged 77.

Morgan, George Charles

Millbrook Place, Little Mill

Born in the Pontypool area in 1885, George is listed on the 1911 census as a Sheet Steel Worker living at Millbrook Place, Little Mill.

George is recorded on the Absent Voters List of 1918 as serving with the King's Liverpool Regiment. However, the service number given actually matches Alfred Morgan, also of Millbrook Place, who is missing from the same list. Therefore, it is not possible to confirm George's service details and it is likely that an error was made when the Absent Voters List was compiled, confusing him with Alfred Morgan. George married in 1928 and died in 1939, aged 55.

Morgan, Ernest Oliver. Private, 1869, 44th Battalion, Australian Imperial Force

Glanusk Farm, near Chain Bridge
British War Medal, Victory Medal

Baptised at St Peter's church on 26th June 1881, Ernest was the son of William and Sarah Morgan of Glanusk Farm, near Chain Bridge. He was one of six brothers who emigrated to Australia. A newspaper article of 18th February 1910 details a farewell party at the Refreshment Rooms, Nantyderry (now the Foxhunter Inn) for Stanley Morgan of Glanusk and notes that the five preceding brothers had found success in Australia.

Ernest became a farmer and enlisted at Perth, Western Australia for the Australian Imperial Force on 23rd March 1916. He was killed in action on 8th June 1917. Ernest's body was not recovered and he is remembered on the Menin Gate and on memorials at St Peter's church and in Boddington, Western Australia.

Morgan, Ira Charles. Private, 14996, 7th Battalion South Wales Borderers

Pontypool
1914 Star, British War Medal, Victory Medal

Born in Pontypool in 1894, Ira was another cousin of William Morgan of Pwllmeyric. A colliery lamp cleaner in Ebbw Vale in 1911 he joined the Army on 3rd September 1914. Serving with the 7th Battalion, South Wales Borderers he arrived in France on 5th September 1915, was later transferred to the 12th Battalion South Wales Borderers, wounded twice and discharged on 17th May 1918. Ira died in 1964.

Morgan, John William. Corporal, 8088, Army Pay Corps

Pencroesoped House

John, of Pencroesoped House, enlisted for the Army Pay Corps on 11th December 1915 and served until 18th March 1919. Nothing more is known about him.

Morgan, Lewis Earl. Private, 364th Infantry, US Army

Concordia, Kansas, United States

Born in Concordia, Kansas, United States in 1890, Lewis was the son of William Morgan, who with his brother Azariah had emigrated from Goytre to Kansas in the early 1880s. Lewis was the cousin to William Morgan of Pwllmeyric and Azariah and Ulysses Morgan of Kansas.

Moving to Los Angeles, Lewis enlisted in the United States Army and served in France with A Company, 364th Infantry, 91st Division.

Lewis was killed in action in the Argonne Forest on 26th September 1918, the first day of the Meuse-Argonne Offensive. This was part of the final push by the Allied forces and cost the US Army 26,000 soldiers. Lewis is commemorated on the Saron Chapel memorial.

Morgan, Richard H. Royal Welsh Fusiliers and Northumberland Fusiliers

Millbrook Place, Little Mill
British War Medal, Victory Medal

It has not been possible to fully trace Richard. He served initially with the Royal Welsh Fusiliers before transferring to the Northumberland Fusiliers. Receiving the British War Medal only, he did not serve in an operational theatre and most likely spent his war in India on garrison service. On the 1918 Absent Voters List he is recorded as living at Millbrook Place, Little Mill.

Morgan, Ulysses Grant. US Army

Cloud County, Kansas

The son of Goytre migrant Azariah Morgan, Ulysses was born in Cloud County, Kansas, United States in 1896. He was the brother of Azariah Decimus Morgan and the cousin of William Morgan of Pwllmeyric.

Ulysses enlisted in the United States Army in 1916, serving under General Pershing in raids on Mexico, and then for almost a year in Europe. He visited his Goytre relatives while awaiting his return to the United States following the end of the war; his father had previously visited in 1909. Ulysses died in Nebraska in 1990, aged 94.

Morgan, William. Lance Corporal, 2257745, 1st Battalion Monmouthshire Regiment

Pen Ty, Rhyd-y-meirch

William Morgan of Pen Ty served with the Monmouthshire Regiment. Nothing more is known about him.

Morgan, William. Sergeant, 2288, 2nd Battalion Monmouthshire Regiment

Pwllmeyric, off Saron Road, Penperlleni
1914 Star, British War Medal, Victory Medal

William was born in Goytre in 1892. On the 1901 census he is listed as living at Pwllmeyric with his parents, Thomas and Jane and siblings Horace, Henry, Ethel and David.

William enlisted on 7th September 1914, joining the 2nd Battalion Monmouthshire Regiment and arrived in France on 7th November 1914. William was promoted to Sergeant and survived the war, being discharged from the Regimental Depot on 24th April 1918, due to wounds received on the Somme. His name is recorded on the Saron Baptist Chapel war memorial.

Returning home, William married Jennie Bishop with whom he had 11 children. He was employed first with a local gas company and then as an insurance agent. During the Second World War he served as a Captain in the local Home Guard unit. He also lost his son Billy (pictured with his father in the photo above), a Rear Gunner with RAF Bomber Command, who was killed when his Handley Page Halifax was lost during the first major raid over Magdeburg in 1944.

William died in 1957, aged 65. He was cousin of several Morgans in the United States and the nephew of David Hugh Morgan.

Morris, B

Listed as survivor on the memorial at St Peter's, he cannot be positively identified in records.

Morris, E

Listed as survivor on the memorial at St Peter's, he cannot be positively identified in records.

Morris, S

Probably Joseph Sidney Morris who was born on 17th December 1894 and baptised at St Peter's church on 27th January 1895. On several records that match his birth date his forename is just given as Sidney. On his baptism record the family residence is given as Goytre Hall where his father was a Labourer.

Sidney attended Goytre School between 1899 and 1907; the school register first records that he lived at Old Stores, Mamhilad, the 1901 census then places him at Yew Tree Cottage.

By 1911 Sidney was a Stable Boy living at Goytre House. Due to his common name it has not been possible to trace his military service. He is recorded as a survivor on the memorial at St Peter's church.

Morris, Valentine Evan. Private, 52777, 1st Battalion Welsh Regiment

Glan Y Nant, Mamhilad
British War Medal, Victory Medal

Valentine was born in Goytre on 14th February 1887 and was baptised at St Peter's church on 13th March. By 1901 he was living with his family at Penwern Cottage, Penperlleni. Penwern Cottages were built on the site of the former 19th century Goytrey poor house, called Nyth Catty (Catty's Nest). Valentine later that year entered employment as a Clerk's Lad at Blaenavon railway station but resigned in 1902. By 1911 he was employed as a painter and was living at Glan Y Nant.

Valentine served with the 1st Battalion, Welsh Regiment and survived the war. He was discharged from service on 14th May 1919 suffering with influenza, malaria and bronchial pneumonia. He died in early 1928, aged 41 whilst living at Ash Cottage, next to the Old Stores, Mamhilad and was buried at St Peter's Church on 25th March.

Parsons, A

Listed as survivor on the memorial at St Peter's, he cannot be positively identified in records.

Parsons, Albert Victor. Lance Corporal, 13841, 8th Battalion Royal Welsh Fusiliers

Yew Tree Cottage, Llanvair
1914/15 Star, British War Medal, Victory Medal

Albert was baptised at St Peter's church on 28th July 1895, the son of George and Catherine of Llanvair Grange where his father was a coachman. The Grange was later the home of Sir Harry Llewellyn who achieved fame as a show jumping champion. With his horse, Foxhunter, he won the only Gold medal for Great Britain at the 1952 Summer Olympics in Helsinki.

By 1911 Albert was a railway worker living at Yew Tree Cottage, Llanvair. He enlisted at Wrexham for the Royal Welsh Fusiliers and arrived with them in the Balkans on 28th June 1915,

Albert was killed in action at Kut, Iraq on 9th April 1916 and is remembered on the Basra memorial as well as on the memorial at St Peter's church.

Parsons, G

Listed as survivor on the memorial at St Peter's, he cannot be positively identified in records.

Parsons, W

Listed as survivor on the memorial at St Peter's, he cannot be positively identified in records.

Phillips, Arthur Thomas. Private, 73727, Liverpool Regiment & Labour Corps

Goytre Wharf
British War Medal, Victory Medal

Arthur was baptised at Llangattock-Juxta-Usk on 9th June 1889 and by 1891 he was living with his family at Yew Tree Cottage, Lower Llanover. His father Francis was a railway platelayer. By 1911 Arthur was a wagoner on a farm near Abergavenny. During the war he served with both the Liverpool Regiment and the Labour Corps. The 1918 Absent Voters List gives his address as Goytre Wharf.

Arthur survived the war and returned home but died in 1923, aged only 33. His name is recorded as a survivor on the memorial at St Peter's church. Arthur was the brother of Francis and Ivor Phillips.

Phillips, Charles. 75010, Private, 5th Battalion Royal Welsh Fusiliers

New Buildings, Croes y pant
British War Medal, Victory Medal

Born in Mamhilad in 1881, he is listed on the 1901 census as a 22 year old Farmer's Son. Due to his common name it has not been possible to uncover anything else about his life. On the 1918 Absent Voters List he is recorded as living at New Buildings, Croes y pant.

Phillips, Herbert Major. Corporal, 266096, Royal Army Medical Corps

Glebe Cottage, Mamhilad
1914/15 Star, British War Medal, Victory Medal

Herbert (whose middle name is also an Army rank) was born in Griffithstown on 23rd January 1885. In 1901 he is recorded as a 16 year old clerk at Mountain Ash railway station and on the 1911 census he is listed as a Labourer living at Bridge Street, Griffithstown.

During the Great War, Herbert served with the Royal Army Medical Corps and was later transferred to the Royal Engineers, achieving the rank of Corporal. He is listed on the Absent Voters List of 1918 as living at Glebe Cottage, Mamhilad.

On the 1939 register he is listed as a Steel Works Foreman living in Pontypool. Herbert died in early 1955 in the Abergavenny area, aged 70.

Phillips, Ivor Charles. Private, 3382, 2nd Battalion Monmouthshire Regiment

Goytre Wharf
British War Medal, Victory Medal

Born on 2nd March 1897, Ivor was the brother of Arthur and James Phillips. By 1911 he was working as a Wagoner's Boy and living at Goytre Wharf.

Serving with the 2nd Battalion, Monmouthshire Regiment, Ivor survived the war and is listed as such on the St Peter's memorial. By 1939 he was living at Wharf Cottage where he worked as an Engineering Canal Labourer.

Arthur died in early 1950, aged 52 and was buried on 27th February at Llangattock-Juxta-Usk.

Phillips, James Francis. Private, South Wales Borderers & Agricultural Company Labour Corps

Goytre Wharf

Francis was baptised at Llangattock-Juxta-Usk on 19th August 1885 and was the brother of Arthur and Ivor Phillips. He enlisted for the South Wales Borderers at Newport on 11th December 1915, giving his next of kin as his father Francis, of Goytre Wharf and employment as Farm Labourer.

James, who enlisted under the Derby Scheme, was transferred to the Army Reserve and was mobilised in March 1916, when his age and marital status group was called forward to serve. He was posted to 422 Agricultural Company at Cardiff on 30th June 1917 and served with various Labour units until discharge in September 1919.

Like his brothers he is listed as a survivor on the memorial at St Peter's church. James died locally in 1956, aged 71.

Pinfield, Frederick Bertram. R/38020, Lance Corporal, 13th Battalion King's Royal Rifle Corps

Goytre Hall
British War Medal, Victory Medal

Frederick Bertram Pinfield was born in Goytre in 1881 and was baptised at St Peter's church on 20th November of that year. He was the second child of Henry George Pinfield and his wife Emily. Frederick's father had started work in the Signals Division of the Great Western Railway in Swindon, at the age of 14. By 1879, when he married Emily in Goytre, he was working as a Telegraph Clerk. At the time of the 1881 census, Henry and Emily were living at Goytre Hall with Emily's sister Jane and widowed father, John Jones, who as well as being a farm labourer was the parish clerk.

By 1901 the family were living in Chippenham, Wiltshire. They were still there in 1911, at 47 Marshfield Road, by which time Frederick was working as a Commercial Traveller. On the night the census was taken, the family had a visitor staying with them, Rosa Buckland aged 27, from Doncaster. Frederick married Rosa in Doncaster the following year.

The rest of Frederick's life is described in detail in Richard Broadhead's book 'Chippenham Soldiers':

Frederick, known as Bert was the eldest son of Henry and Emily Pinfield and was first educated at St Paul's School and then completed his education at the North Wilts Technical College at Swindon. At the age of 16 years he gained employment with the Collen Brothers at Chippenham Flour Mills, initially as a clerk, before being promoted to outdoor representative and was employed with them for twenty years.

Bert also had a great love of sport, he was Captain of Chippenham Football Club for several years before becoming a referee. He was a keen cricketer being a skilful batsman and played a good game of tennis.

He helped form the Amateur Dramatic Society and was a member of St Paul's Church choir and regularly took part in the services.

In 1912 Bert married Rosa Gertrude Buckland at Doncaster and the couple set up home in Chippenham. At the outbreak of hostilities, Bert joined the Wiltshire Volunteers (home guard) and was in the cycle section; he was described as a skilful marksman. Bert was called up joining the Army Service Corps but was transferred to the 13th Kings Royal Rifle Corps and was sent to France in February 1917 while also being promoted to Lance Corporal. He took part in the fighting at Arras and on Saturday 29th September 1917 the 13th KRRC were near Polygon Wood East of Ypres Belgium.

In early October 1917 Rosa Pinfield received the following letter from a Captain, Bert's company commanding officer. "I am very sorry to have to inform you of the death of your husband who was a non commissioned officer in the company in which I command. I only wish to say something to soften the shock of the sad news for you, but at such times words from anyone are little good. I can only hope that in the course of time the fact that he made the supreme sacrifice in the fight for freedom of the future generations may help you a little. Your husband was killed by a shell this morning at 6.45, during a heavy bombardment; he was only a few yards away from me at the time, in our trenches. I do not think he could have had time to realise he was even hit. You may feel glad, therefore, that he suffered no agony or physical pain. I had recommended your husband for a commission and he was expected very shortly to return to England for his course of training. I can only assure you of the sympathy felt by the whole of his company with you in your loss. Your husband was very popular with all his comrades."

Bert had written the following in a letter prior to his death:

"As you say, it is in the hands of God. I believe when I go over the great divide I am going to a better place, and I don't want any funeral music sung for me".

The following appeared in the Wiltshire Times on 13th Oct 1917

Well-Known Footballer Killed in action

Mr and Mrs Pinfield of Landsend, on Friday received the sad intelligence that their son Bertram had been killed in action. The news will be received with great regret by all who knew Bert, as he was familiarly called, not only in Chippenham but over a wide part of the county where he took a great interest in sport. He was a well-known member of the Chippenham football and cricket clubs and was an able exponent of both games. In the football team he was one of the forwards, was an official referee of the County Football Association and a general favourite. Prior to joining up he was a traveller for Messieurs Collen Bros., Chippenham Mills. For several years he was a member of the choir at St Paul's church and those associated with him there and elsewhere deeply deplore his death. Deceased who was 36 years of age was married to a daughter of Mr Buckland of Audley Road. He leaves a widow and 1 child and with her and his parents and relatives there is much sympathy. Mr HG Pinfield (the father) is chairman of the Wiltshire Football league and a member of the Council of Wiltshire Football Association.

Another article was printed on 27th Oct.

A memorial service for L/Cpl Bertram Pinfield was held at St Paul's Church on Sunday afternoon. A large congregation included Councillor and Mrs Pinfield, the Mayor and Mayoress. Bertram had been a member of the choir for about 25 years, before he enlisted. He was killed on September 29 1917.

Frederick's body was not recovered, and he is commemorated on Tyne Cot Memorial. In the late 1980s/early 1990s a new housing estate was built at Pewsham to form part of Chippenham. Several roads were named after local Great War casualties, including Pinfield Lane.

Probert, A.

Bridge Farm, Saron Road, Penperlleni

Probably the Alfred Probert who was born in Herefordshire on 4th January 1895, and by 1911 was living at Bridge Farm, Goytre and employed as a Plasterer's Apprentice. Nothing can be discovered about his military service, but his name is recorded as a survivor on the memorial at St Peter's church.

Alfred married on 19th April 1919 at St Peter's church to Emily Boyce, also of Goytre and by 1939 was living in Monkswood and working as an Automobile Association Patrolman. Alfred died in the Pontypool area in the autumn of 1972, aged 77.

Powles, Arthur William. 30075, Private, 4th Battalion South Wales Borderers

Lower Pentwyn Farm, Nantyderry
British War Medal, Victory Medal

Born in Cwmyoy on 6th May 1888, by 1911 Arthur was employed as a farm worker at Lower Pentwyn Farm. On 12th July 1915 he married Eva Walker of Penwern, at St Peter's church.

Serving with the 4th Battalion, South Wales Borderers, Arthur survived the war and returned to Goytre following his discharge on 29th March 1919. His name is listed as a survivor on the memorial at St Peter's.

Eva died in 1925, aged 32 and Arthur remarried on 30th October 1929 at St Peter's to Gladys Rogers of Llantrisant. On the marriage record he gave his address as Sunny Bank, Penperlleni. He was still living at Sunny Bank in 1939 and working as a Builders Labourer. Arthur died in the local area in late 1969, aged 81.

Richards, Llewellyn Thomas. Lieutenant, 17th Battalion Royal Welsh Fusiliers

Y Gwynydd, Penperlleni
British War Medal, Victory Medal

Llewellyn was born in Pontllanfraith in 1899. His father William was a Sub Postmaster and his mother, Rachel, was originally from Mamhilad.

Commissioned as an officer in the Royal Welsh Fusiliers, Llewellyn was killed near Bapaume on 5th September 1918 whilst his Battalion was preparing to launch an attack.

He was buried at Morval British Cemetery and is also remembered on a plaque erected by his mother at Capel Ed Chapel. On the 1918 Absent Voters List his address was given as Y Gwynydd, Goytre.

Robinson, Walter James. G/19185, Private, 7th Battalion East Kent Regiment

Lincolnshire & Newport
British War Medal, Victory Medal

Born in Lincolnshire, Walter was the fiancé of Muriel, the daughter of the Reverend Joseph Davies of St Peter's Church. By 1911 he was a boarder at 51 Risca Road, Newport and employed as a Bank Cashier for Lloyds. Walter was killed in action on 12th October 1917, aged 37, serving with the East Kent Regiment. He has a plaque dedicated to him at St Peter's church and is also remembered on the Tyne Cot Memorial, the Newport Town Roll of Honour and on the Newport Athletic Club memorial. A series of letters between the Davies and Robinson families following Walter's death has survived and is transcribed in Appendix B.

Rogers, Abraham.

Horseshoe Inn, Mamhilad

Abraham was born in Pontypool on 22nd April 1896. He attended Goytre School between 1901 and 1909 and then progressed to West Monmouth School. On the 1911 census he is listed living with his family at the Horseshoe Inn (pictured left), Mamhilad and working as an Apprentice Carpenter. The Absent Voters List does not list either his unit or service number and it is not possible to identify him from other military records.

On the 1939 Register, Abraham is listed as still living at the Horseshoe Inn and working as a General Building Repairer. He died in Cornwall in 1971, aged 75.

Rogers, J

Listed as a survivor on the memorial at Saron Baptist Chapel, nothing is known about him.

Rosser, Robert John. 52854, Private, 8th Battalion Welsh Regiment

Beech Cottage, Saron Road, Penperlleni
British War Medal, Victory Medal

Robert was born in Goytre on 1st November 1884 and by 1901 he was living at Guild Garn. He married at St Peter's Church on 30th July 1914, to May Harding, also of Goytre.

He enlisted for the Army at Newport on 13th November 1916, giving his occupation as Carpenter and Sign Writer. Serving with the 8th Battalion, Welsh Regiment he sailed from Devonport on 17th January 1917 and arrived in India on 17th March 1918. Later serving in Salonica and Turkey, Robert retuned on the UK on 14 September 1919 and was discharged from the Army three months later

On leaving the Army Robert returned to his home at Beech Cottage, near Saron Baptist Chapel. His name is recorded as survivor on the memorial at St Peter's church. He later applied for an Army pension due to a defective right ear, which Robert claimed was as a result of his war service. He was examined in Cardiff in November 1919 but his issue was diagnosed as wax and his claim was rejected.

By 1939 Robert was working as a Sign Writer and Coach Painter and still living at Beech Cottage. He died at the Royal Gwent Hospital in Newport on 3rd May 1965 aged 80.

Rosser, William George. 43990, Gunner, Royal Field Artillery

Millbrook Place, Little Mill
Queen's South Africa Medal, British War Medal, Victory Medal

Born in Panteg on 18th June 1873, William first enlisted for the Royal Field Artillery in Newport on 5th August 1892. In June 1893 he was subject of a Court of Enquiry to determine the cause of an accident in which he was injured. His finger had been crushed and fractured by a falling box when unloading a wagon outside the Battery office.

Serving in the UK until 1899, William saw action in the Boer War in South Africa for which he received the Queen's South Africa Medal. He returned to the UK in August 1900 and served until his discharge in 1908, returning to his trade as a Platelayer.

William married in Pontypool in 1905 to Lydia and on the 1911 census they are living at Lower New Inn, Pontypool. He re-enlisted for the Royal Field Artillery at Newport on 10th April 1915, at the age of 41, giving his employment as Platelayer and address as Millbrook Place, Little Mill. William served in the UK until 27th November 1917 and then embarked for service in France. He survived the war and returned home.

By 1939 William was living at 57 Commercial Street, Pontypool and still working as a Platelayer. He died in the Pontypool area in 1948, aged 74.

Scrivens, Charles. 36701, Private, South Wales Borderers

Millbrook Place, Little Mill

Charles was born in 1878 and was a 38 year old labourer living at Millbrook Place, Little Mill when he enlisted at Newport on 29th November 1915. He was placed on the Army Reserve and mobilised on 14th March 1916. Charles was discharged just weeks later, on 26th June 1916, due to pulmonary tuberculosis. He died in 1918, aged just 40.

Skillern, Charles. Gunner, 190729, Royal Field Artillery

Millbrook Place, Little Mill
British War Medal, Victory Medal

Born on 31st December 1897, Charles is recorded on the 1911 census as a schoolboy living at Millbrook Place, Little Mill. He was the brother of George and William Skillern. Charles attended Glascoed and Mamhilad Schools.

During the Great War, Charles served with the Royal Field Artillery, arriving overseas after the start of 1916, receiving the British War Medal and Victory Medal.

Charles' descendants recall that upon leaving the Army he became a policeman, later manning the gate at the Royal Ordnance Factory in Glascoed. In 1924 he was presented with a clock in recognition for his actions in an unknown incident.

He was still living in Millbrook Place when the 1939 Register was taken and by then was a Stationary Engine Driver. He is also noted as being a Special Constable. Charles died in the Pontypool area in 1963, aged 65.

Skillern, George Henry. 1334, Private, 2nd Battalion Monmouthshire Regiment

Millbrook Place, Little Mill
1914 Star, British War Medal, Victory Medal

Born on 1st August 1890, George was the brother of Charles Skillern and William Skillern. He is listed with his brothers living at Millbrook Place on the 1911 census.

Like his brother William, George was a pre-war Territorial with the 2nd Battalion Monmouthshire Regiment. They possibly even enlisted together, with George's service number being only three lower than his brother's. Arriving with the Battalion in France on 7th November 1914, George was later transferred to the Machine Gun Corps and survived the war.

On the 1939 Register, George is listed as living in Abergavenny and working as a Stationary Engine Stoker. He died in the Abergavenny area in 1941, aged 50.

Skillern, William Thomas. 1337, Private, 2nd Battalion Monmouthshire Regiment

Millbrook Place, Little Mill
1914 Star, British War Medal, Victory Medal

William was born in the Pontypool area on 24th May 1892. By 1911 he was living at Millbrook Place, Little Mill with his brothers Charles and George and was employed as a Brickyard Labourer.

A pre-war Territorial with the 2nd Battalion Monmouthshire Regiment, he served in France from 7th November 1914, but was discharged from the Army on 3rd December 1915 as a result of sickness.

William married in Narberth, Pembrokeshire in 1925 and by 1939 was a General Labourer living in Blaenau Ffestiniog. He died there in 1956, aged 63.

Smith, James. 51791, Sapper, Royal Engineers

Monkswood
1914/15 Star, British War Medal, Victory Medal

Born in Monkswood, James was a 34 year old bricklayer when he enlisted at Newport on 7th September 1914. He re-joined the Royal Engineers, which he had previously served five years with before purchasing his discharge.

Posted to a Field Company, James served in France from May 1915 and survived the war. He was discharged on 30th March 1919, giving his address as 1 Prospect Place, Upper Pontnewydd. Nothing more is known of his life.

Summers, William John. Private, Labour Corps

Yew Tree Cottage, Penpedairheol

William was born in Goytre on 8th September 1890 and was educated at Goytre School between 1895 and 1903. By 1911 he was a Plasterer living at Yew Tree Cottage, Penpedairheol.

Serving with the Labour Corps William survived the war and returned home. His name is recorded as a survivor on the St Peter's memorial.

By 1939 he was a Market Gardener living at Lime Tree Cottage, Pontypool. William died in the Pontypool area in 1957, aged 66.

Stinchcombe, George Francis. 22457, Lance Corporal, South Wales Borderers & Royal Engineers

Nutshell, Penperlleni
1914/15 Star, British War Medal, Victory Medal

George was born on 12th May 1886 and, at the time of his enlistment at Newport on 1st June 1915, he was living at 24 Lewis Street, Crumlin. He also declared previous service as a Territorial.

Initially serving with the 11th Battalion, South Wales Borderers, George was transferred to the Royal Engineers on 30th January 1916. He then spent the majority of his remaining service with Special Works units as a carpenter.

George survived the war and upon discharge in January 1919 gave his address as Nutshell, Goytre. By 1939 he was a Bricklayer living at Prioress Mill, Llanbadoc, Usk. George was also a member of the St John's Ambulance Brigade during WW2. Nothing more is known of his life.

Thomas, W. Sergeant, 2nd Battalion Monmouthshire Regiment

Listed as a survivor of the 2nd Battalion, Monmouthshire Regiment on the memorial at Saron Baptist Chapel. Nothing more is known about him.

Thomas, William John. 31176, Lance Corporal, Machine Gun Corps

Llanover Estate
British War Medal, Victory Medal

Born in Cwmavon on 23rd September 1889, William was the eldest son of William and Mary Anne Thomas of Chepstow Hill Farm, Caerleon. He was educated at Caerleon School before entering service as a Gardener at Llanover Estate.

In January 1913 William gave up his employment and entered Coleg Trefeca, Talgarth as a candidate for the Welsh Presbyterian Church.

Enlisting for the Royal Welsh Fusiliers (although his obituary incorrectly states South Wales Borderers) on 8th February 1916, he was transferred to the Machine Gun Corps and served in France from 31st July 1916.

William died of wounds at No 53 Casualty Clearing Station on 6th October 1916, aged 27. Buried in the Doullens Communal Cemetery in France, a brass plaque dedicated to his memory was unveiled at Capel Ed, Penperlleni on 20th December of that year. This was only a little over ten months after he had enlisted. He is also remembered on the Christchurch war memorial in Newport.

The following was printed in the Brecon & Radnor Express.

"Trevecca has again sent her students to the war. One of them, Lance-Corporal Willie Thomas, has been killed. He joined the South Wales Borderers early this year and was transferred to the Machine Gun Corps. He was the son of Mr and Mrs Wm. Thomas, Chepstow Hill Farm, Caerleon, and, prior to entering Trevecca, was engaged on Llanover Estate at Goytre. At Trevecca he gave promise that he would become a successful minister and his death is mourned, not only by his friends and relatives, but throughout the de- nomination. His brother, Ralph, is serving in the British Navy."

Turfrey, John. M2/203289, Private, Army Service Corps

Pentovy Place, Little Mill
British War Medal, Victory Medal

No census records can be found for anyone with this name in Monmouthshire. John served overseas after the start of 1916 and his medal index card gives a Brecon address, so he is possibly the John Turfrey who died in Brecknockshire in 1930, aged 38. Listed on the 1918 Absent Voters List as living at Pentovy Place, Little Mill.

Wall MSM, Frank Edward. 1339, Warrant Officer Class II, 2nd Battalion Monmouthshire Regiment

Mamhilad School
1914 Star, British War Medal, Victory Medal, Meritorious Service Medal

Frank Edward Wall was born in Radnor on 26th June 1885 and was the brother of George Wilfred Wall. On the 1911 census he is recorded as a Corrugator in Iron Works, living at Mamhilad Council School, where his sister Harriet was an Assistant Teacher. He had previously been employed by the Great Western Railway at Tredegar station. A pre-war Territorial with the 2nd Battalion, Monmouthshire Regiment, Frank arrived in France on 7th November 1914. He became one of only a handful of men who remained with the Battalion right through until the end of the war and reached the rank of Warrant Officer Class II. On 30th June 1918 it was recorded in the Battalion war diary that Frank had been awarded the Meritorious Service Medal. He was one of a number of soldiers from the Battalion presented with medal ribbons by the Commanding Officer of the 29th Division on 3rd July 1918.

Surviving the war, Frank returned home and is believed to have died in the Newport area in 1961.

Wall, George Wilfred. 199378, Gunner, Royal Field Artillery

Bay Tree House, Croes yn y pant

Born in Radnor on 16th June 1882 and the brother of Frank Edward Wall, George is recorded on the 1911 census as living in Mamhilad and working as a Packer in the Galvanised Works.

George joined the Army on 28th March 1918 and served until his discharge on 5th December 1918, due to illness. He did not serve overseas and therefore did not receive any medals. The 1918 Absent Voters List lists him living at Bay Tree House, Croes yn y pant (present day Croes y pant).

On the 1939 register George is recorded as living in Pontypool and working as a Sheetworker. Nothing more is known about his life.

Walton, George. 186020, Gunner, Royal Garrison Artillery

New House, Saron Lane, Penperlleni
British War Medal, Victory Medal

Born in Newport on 7th January 1896, George is listed on the 1911 census as an Assistant Gardener living with his family at New House, Goytre. During the war George served with the Royal Garrison Artillery. He survived the war and on the 1918 Absent Voters List his address is given as Goytre Cottage, Penperlleni. Nothing more is known of his life.

Westlake, Ernest James. 61780, Private, 16th Battalion, South Lancashire Regiment

Rose Cottage, Goytre

Believed to have been from Exeter, he was working as a miner in Risca in 1911. The 1918 Absent Voters List gives his address as Rose Cottage, Goytre. There are a number of Rose Cottages in the area, and it is not known which particular one this is. Nothing more is known about him.

71

Whitehead, Lionel Digby. Captain, 3rd Battalion Monmouthshire Regiment

Goytre Hall
1914/15 Star, British War Medal, Victory Medal

Lionel Whitehead was born in Yorkshire in 1878 and was the son of a JP. By 1911 he was an Ironmaster living in Tredegar with his wife and household. On 25th February 1914, he arrived in New York as a passenger on-board SS Olympic before travelling onto Pittsburgh. She was a sister ship to the Titanic and acted as a troopship in WW1, earning the nickname 'Old Reliable'.

Lionel was commissioned as a 2nd Lieutenant in the Monmouthshire Regiment on 9th September 1914 and arrived in France with the 3rd Battalion in February 1915. The address given on his medal card is Goytre Hall, Abergavenny. During his absence his wife was instrumental in the local effort on the home front, organising parcels to send to the front line.

Lionel survived the war and returned to Goytre Hall and co-authored the book 'On the Western Front – 1/3 Battalion Monmouthshire Regiment'. He is also listed as a survivor on the memorial at St Peter's church. Later Deputy Lord Lieutenant of Monmouthshire, he died in Brecknockshire in early 1938, aged 60.

Williams, Alfred. Royal Monmouthshire Royal Engineers

Fir Tree Cottage

No trace can be found of Alfred or his service records. On the 1918 Absent Voters List he is recorded as living at Fir Tree Cottage.

Williams, Arthur J. 265700, Private, 2nd Battalion Monmouthshire Regiment

Old Stores, Mamhilad
1914/15 Star, British War Medal, Victory Medal

Little is known about Arthur due to his common name. Serving with the 2nd Battalion, Monmouthshire Regiment, Albert arrived in France on 17th February 1915 and survived the war, being discharged on 9th October 1918 as a result of wounds. On the 1918 Absent Voters List his address is recorded as The Old Stores, Mamhilad.

Williams, Ernest E. 2990, Guardsman, 2nd Battalion Welsh Guards

Keeper's Cottage, Mamhilad
British War Medal, Victory Medal

Ernest was born in the local area in 1883 and by the time of his enlistment in 1915 was living with his wife and two children at Keeper's Cottage, Mamhilad.

Joining the Army under the Derby Scheme on 9th December 1915, Ernest was mobilised on 17th August 1916 and was posted to the 2nd Battalion, Welsh Guards, joining them in France on 20th February 1917. Ernest was hospitalised several times with bronchitis before being evacuated back to the UK on 15th November 1917. He recovered sufficiently enough to return to action and re-joined his Battalion in France on 1st September 1918.

Ernest survived the war and returned to England on 3rd March 1919 and left the Army on 16th October that year.

Recorded on the 1918 Absent Voters List as living at The Nest but it is not known where this residence is located in Goytre.

The Home Front

The war effort on the Home Front began almost as soon as the first troops mobilised. As reported in the Abergavenny Chronicle on 7th August 1914, Goytre Parish Church had already raised £17 at services the previous Sunday in aid of the National Relief Fund. On 6th November, the day before the 2nd Mons landed in France, the wife of the Commanding Officer, Colonel Cuthbertson, began accepting donations of clothing, tobacco and money in aid of her husband's Battalion. Mrs Cuthbertson was a key figure in local fundraising throughout the entire war; she is again reported in the Abergavenny Chronicle on 16th April 1915 as having donated in aid of sick and injured Army horses.

Another early fundraising drive was in aid of the 250,000 Belgian refugees who had been displaced as a result of the German invasion of their country and had sought sanctuary in Britain. A London based organisation was established to co-ordinate country wide local committees to organise fundraising and to find suitable accommodation for the Belgians. The April 23rd 1915 edition of the Abergavenny Chronicle reports that local donators included Mrs Davies of Goytre (probably the wife of the Revd Joseph Davies of St Peter's), although it is not known if any Belgians were housed in the immediate area; they certainly were at Abergavenny and Crickhowell.

The Red Cross was another organisation that was well supported by Goytre during the war. On 18th February 1915 a patriotic concert and dance was held at Nantyderry School, chaired by the Revd. Davies. Not ending until after midnight the sum of £5 9s was raised. These entertainment evenings were frequent in Goytre during the war; another is reported to have taken place on 2nd December 1915 at Nantyderry school room. Again organised by the Revd. Davies it was reported as follows

GOYTRE. Successful and well attended entertainment (organised by Mrs. Davies, The Rectory) was held at the School- room, in connection with the Parish Church, on Thursday evening, the 2nd inst., in aid of War Funds. It was, without doubt, one of the most pleasant and successful concerts held in the Schoolroom for many years, and reflected great credit upon all who took part. The following contributed to the programme:—Miss Hughes (Nantyderry House), Mrs. E. Evans (The Goytrey), Mrs. Jackson and Miss Williams (Abergavenny), Misses Davies (Griffithstown),

74

Miss V. Harding (Nantyderry), Mr. Percy Jones, Mr. C. Harris. Mr. C. Merrick, and Messrs. Horsington. During the evening, the sketch, "Biddy from Cork," was well performed by Misses Davies (Rectory), Miss Wilks, Mrs. Jones (New Barn), Mrs. Leworthy and Mrs. Titcombe, and caused great amusement. The Rector presided, and at the close thanked all who had so willingly helped. Light refreshments (given by several friends) were sold at very moderate charges

The Mr C. Merrick is undoubtably Charles Merrick of Feltham Cottage, who later served in the Army Service Corps and for many years was a local music teacher and organist at St Peter's.

Goytre put so much effort into fundraising that it was decided that money raised from the Parish Fete held in early June 1916 would be used to put the committee into a strong financial position, rather than donate to the war effort as per the previous year. Again the report in the Abergavenny Chronicle lists a number of villagers:

Those in charge were as follows: — Jumble stall—Miss Byrde, Miss Clougher and Miss Wood. Fancy stall—Mrs. Davies and Miss Davies (the Rectory). Sweet stall—Misses G. and A. Gwatkin. Cake stall—Mrs. Evan Jones, Miss Wilks, and Miss G. Harding. Flower stall—Mssss Harris. Ice cream stall—Miss Gwen Bamfield. Bran tub–Miss Ella Bamfield. Aunt Sally—Mr. C. Cornish and Mr. Joe Owen. Shooting gallery and bagatelles—Mr. J. Rosser and Mr. Evan Gwatkin. The Little Mill Reformatory Band was present, and under the conductorship of Band- master Allen played pleasing selections in a very creditable manner, when the weather permitted. Tea was served in the Schoolroom, the ladies presiding at the tables being Mrs. Jenkins (the Mill), Mrs. Jenkins (New Barn), Mrs. Morris, Mrs. J. Owen and Mrs. Arthur Jenkins, who were assisted by a number of young ladies in the cutting-up department, and by Mr. George Jones. Several competitions were held Miss Victoria Jenkins winning the prize for the best bunch of garden flowers, and the Rector (the Rev. Joseph Davies) calculating most nearly the number of peas in a bottle. The weather cleared up in the evening and the conditions were more enjoyable, though the wet state of the ground prevented anything in the nature of sports.

However, the committee evidently had a change of heart and it was later reported that the Fete raised £5 for the Red Cross.

The following year the fete funds were used to both donate to the war effort and to contribute to church expenses, as reported in the Abergavenny Chronicle on 15th June 1917

GOYTRE SALE OF WORK. SUCCESSFUL EFFORT FOR WAR
FUNDS AND CHURCH EXPENSES.

The parochial events held at Goytre are invariably successful, and the sale of work, jumble sale, etc., held on Thursday last was no exception to the rule. The event, which was in aid of church expenses and war funds, was held at the Nantyderry Schoolroom and in the field adjoining, the latter being kindly lent by Mrs. Gwatkin, Church Farm. The arrangements had been made by the Rector (the Rev. Joseph Davies), the churchwardens, Messrs. Richard Jenkins and W. Jenkins, Mrs. Davies (the Rectory), Miss Byrde, and Miss Wilks. The stalls in the schoolroom comprised the stall of useful articles, in charge of Mrs. Davies and the Misses Davies (the Rectory), the Jumble Stall in charge of Miss Byrde. Miss Clougher, Miss Wood and Miss Maggie Boyce, and the Bag Stall, in charge of Miss Wilks and Miss Hobbiss. In the field were the following stalls.—Flower Stall, Misses Harris and Miss Ivy Jenkins: Refreshment Stall, Mrs. Jenkins (the Mill), Mrs. I Jenkins (Ty-coch), Mrs. Leworthy, Mrs. Collins, Mrs. J. Owen, and Miss Banfield Sweet Stall, Mr. Dalby and Misses Sophie and Amy Gwatkin. Aunt Sally," Messrs. J. Owen and Franklin Harris bran tub, Miss M. J. Evans. Mr. Logan, of Llanover, was present with his bag-pipes, on which he played selections during the afternoon and evening. Mr. W. Cornish also gave selections on the gramophone. Mr. Roger Morgan (Lower House) kindly lent the use of his donkey, on which the children enjoyed rides at a penny a time. Although for various reasons the proceeds were not expected to be as large as on some former occasions, a substantial sum was realised.

The Gwatkin family of Church Farm who lent their field for the event had a son, Gilbert, serving in the war with an Agricultural Company of the Labour Corps.

Fundraising continued into 1918 with a Whist drive on January 21st as a result of which 12s was donated to the Red Cross. The final mention of Goytre fundraising activity during the war was £1 12s 9d collected at the Sunday service at St Peter's on 4th August 1918 in aid of the Monmouthshire Prisoners of War Fund.

As well as financial contributions the people of Goytre also made many donations of vegetables, fruit and even eggs, as first reported in the Abergavenny Chronicle on 24th September 1915

GOYTREY. EGG COLLECTION.-Another one hundred and seventy-three eggs were collected last Sunday for the National Egg Collection, at St. Peter's Church, Goytrey. Altogether one thousand one hundred and fifty eggs have been brought to the church. The eggs are sent to London, and from there they are sent to the wounded soldiers and sailors.

As the war progressed donations of this nature, including from the Harvest Festival of 1916, were often given to Maindiff Court Red Cross Hospital in Abergavenny to support the recovery of the wounded.

From these reports one can see that Goytre was very much a rural community, rich in farming and agriculture. However, as men left the farms to join the armed forces, the ability to farm the land was reduced. This was compounded further when conscription was introduced on 2nd March 1916, when the Military Services Act (1916) came into force.

Those called up and their employers did have an avenue of appeal through local tribunals; these ruled whether an individual had to report for service, could be exempt, or if their call up had grounds for deference for a set period of time. Several tribunals involved Goytre men. On 21st July 1916 an exemption until the end of October was reported in the Abergavenny Chronicle for an unnamed local man.

A smallholder with 31 acres, at Llanvair and Goytre, stated that he had a wife and four children. In reply to questions, he said he had only been at Llanvair 12 months He had worked in the collieries, but he was brought up on a farm. As the fences were bad he had not ploughed any land yet, but he intended to plough about seven acres. The land was his own freehold, but there was a mortgage on it. Mr. Gower Andrews What stock have you ? Applicant Seven head of cattle, 22 ewes and two horses. Exemption till the end of October was granted

It was reported on 1st June 1917 that another local man, Charles Stinchcombe a blacksmith, had been granted a conditional exemption although the facts of the case are not given.

Frank Alexander, a veteran of the Boer War with the South African Constabulary, may have thought that his previous service for his country would be looked upon sympathetically when he made his appeal. This was reported in the Abergavenny Chronicle on 31st August 1917

COUNTY TRIBUNAL. SIR HENRY MATHER-JACKSON AND AGRICULTURAL CASES.

There was only one local case before the County Appeal Tribunal on Monday. This was the case of Frank Alexander, smallholder and market gardener, of Llanover, who has also been working underground as a timber man for the Blaenavon Company. In this case Mr Homfray Davies (secretary of the Monmouthshire Farmers' Union) attempted to get in a word. The Chairman told him he could not hear him. The agricultural question had been taken out of their hands by the Board of Agriculture, and the cases must either go before the War Agricultural Committee or come direct before them. If they came there, notwithstanding Mr. Davies's official appointment by the Board of Agriculture, then they would refuse to hear him, because he had no locus standi. If the Board of Agriculture were not satisfied he would refer the whole of the cases to that body. They could not go on reviewing the cases and hearing anyone who liked to come there. He would continue to hear Mr. Harding as the representative of the agricultural interest, but as a matter of courtesy (he knew nothing officially of any other appointment) he would hear Mr. Davies in any case which had not been before the War Agricultural Committee. The application was refused, the man to join on October 27th.

Frank subsequently served with the 3rd Hussars and survived the war, later living at Woodland Cottage near Goytre Wharf.

As seen in these cases, tribunals were reluctant to grant exemptions, which placed an even greater strain on the stretched resources on the farms. This in turn this led to women being called upon for land work that they would, in the society of the time, not normally have been involved in.

The Abergavenny Chronicle, on 26th May 1916, reports on the activity of a scheme established in Abergavenny to organise female labour for farms. At that point they had a register of 22 women in the Abergavenny area willing to work at any farm in the district and another 35 who were responsible for running households but were willing to undertake farm labour during the day, at a distance of no more than two miles from their homes. In support of this scheme, farm owners came forward to offer cottages for accommodation for these workers.

Training for volunteers was provided at Usk Agricultural College and at a farm in Nantyderry. Just two months after this article was printed, it was reported that a Miss Cassen had qualified at Nantyderry to wear the green armband of the Board of Agriculture to denote the completion of thirty days work on the land. Agricultural training at Nantyderry continued throughout the war.

Another Goytre connection with the home front is through Dorothy, the wife of Charles Merrick. Prior to their marriage, she was part of the little-known Women's Forage Corps who were active 1915-1920, undertaking jobs such as hay baling, sack making, sheet repairing, thatching, driving tractors and clerical duties. Charles and Dorothy met during the war, with Charles completing his entire service in the UK as an Engineer. He was under orders to proceed to France when the war ended.

Another way in which the village contributed to the war effort was through the use of Goytre House, the grounds of which were utilised as a base by the Army. Unfortunately, little is known about why Goytre House was used or which units were stationed there, and research has not yielded any results. What is known is that the village Blacksmith, Edgar Thomas (pictured left), was contracted by the Army to supply horseshoes for the many horses that the Army had stabled there. This work was undertaken from the smithy (pictured below, in the 1960s), located in the row of cottages opposite the junction of School Lane. The workshop, long since demolished was the first building in the row, when approaching from the direction of the railway bridge at the top of Newtown Road and heading towards the junction with the A4042.

The old smithy with its outbuildings can also be seen in the picture on page 5. Originally the cottages had thatched roofs, as shown in the picture on page 6, but these were set on fire, allegedly, from activity at the smithy. Today's end cottage (abutting the smithy left) is appropriately named Phoenix Cottage.

Schools

The two main schools serving the area at the time of the Great War were Goytre British School and Mamhilad School. Due to the digitisation of historical school registers, it has been possible to identify pupils of these schools who served, although there were possibly more. Those listed in the tables below marked with an asterisk were killed.

Goytre School, early 20th century

Goytre British School was located in School Lane, opposite where the current primary school is, and was opened in 1870 on a site donated by Colonel Byrde at a cost of £600. The building is currently in use as the Goytre Fawr Community Centre. A description from 1891 states that the school could cater for 120 pupils, with 80 being the average attendance. The following pupils have been identified from the registers, which includes the address they were living at when they joined the school:

Name	Address	Years Attended
Lewis Richard Bowen		1893 - 1903
Reginald Cornish	Chapel Ed Cottage	1897 - 1907
George Dobbs*	Abergavenny Road	1896 - 1906
John Dobbs*	Abergavenny Road	1903 - 1913
Gilbert Gwatkin	Church Farm	1904 - 1910
Albert Edward Higgs	Penwern	1902 - 1905
William Thomas Higgs*	Penwern	1902 - 1905

Ernest Humphreys	Penystair	1895 - 1905
Iltyd Charles Jenkins	New Barn	1903 - 1910
Sidney H. Kirby*	Goytre	1895 - 1897
Charles Merrick	Reformatory	1894 - 1903
Benjamin Morgan	Pwllbach	1895 - 1905
Clifford Louis Morgan	Park Bach	1902 - 1910
David Morgan		1874 - ?
Joseph Sidney Morris		1899 - 1907
Valentine Evan Morris	Penwern	1891 - 1899
Abraham Rogers		1901 - 1909
Robert John Rosser		1891 - 1897
William John Summers	Goytre	1895 - 1903

Mamhilad school was built in 1856 on land given by Pontypool Park Estate. The building has been converted to a house since WW2. The following Mamhilad School pupils served:

Name	Address	Years Attended
William Brinkworth	Little Mill	1902 - ?
Charles Skillern	Little Mill	1906 - ?
George Walton	Glebe Cottage	1907- ?

A third school, the Monmouthshire Reformatory, was established in 1859 and was located at Ty Draw, half a mile north of Little Mill. It was originally opened to detain boys sentenced by a magistrate to short terms of imprisonment, typically between two and five years.

By 1891 there were 40 boys being held at the Reformatory. The Schoolmaster in 1891 was Charles Merrick, whose son of the same name served in WW1 and is listed in this book. Each Sunday the boys would be marched to St Matthew's church at Glascoed for the Sunday service.

Of 130 boys from the Reformatory who later served in the Great War, nine were killed. A plaque dedicated to their memory was unveiled at St Matthew's on 23rd March 1922, in the same year[1] that the school was closed. The names of the fallen are listed below but do not appear elsewhere in this book as the individuals were from outside the Goytre area.

---

[1] From Ray Westlake's book First World War Graves and Memorials Volume 2

Name	Address	Years Held	Killed
Charles Brown	London	1913- ?	15/8/1916
Joseph Byng	Birmingham	1909-1913	23/3/1915
Alfred Coombes	Abercarn	1902 -1907	Unknown
Richard Curtis	Birmingham	1912-1914	3/9/1916
Alfred Hammond	Birmingham	1910-1914	14/11/1915
Leonard Head	Salisbury	1911-?	7/11/1914
Arthur Pinfield	Birmingham	1915-?	13/4/1918
Edward Robinson	Salisbury	1913-1916	23/10/1918
Henry Winwood	Blaenavon	1906-1910	21/12/1914

We Will Remember Them

The guns fell silent for the first time in over four years at eleven o'clock on the 11th November 1918. Despite all sides agreeing to cease fighting, it was not until the Treaty of Versailles was signed on 28th June 1919 that the war formally ended, although Britain had already started to demobilise by this point and large numbers of volunteers were returning home.

By the end of the war over twenty men of Goytre had lost their lives (see Appendix A). The last recorded Goytre connected casualty was Lewis Earl Morgan, who fell on 26th September 1918 whilst fighting with the U.S. Army in the Argonne Forest. Lewis was the son of parents who had emigrated to the United States from Goytre. The Morgan family had close ties with the Saron Baptist Chapel, having donated the land it was built on and Lewis was therefore commemorated on the chapel memorial alongside other Morgans.

The last known casualty to have actually lived in Goytre was John Arthur Dobbs of Llwyncelyn Farm, a former pupil of Goytre School. He was killed in action whilst serving with the Machine Gun Corps on 6th July 1918, aged 18. His older brother George Dobbs had been killed two years previously.

Those who returned home did not automatically escape from the horrors of the war with many carrying physical or mental wounds. Many died from conditions, that even if they were not as a direct result of the war, were probably exasperated by it. The former servicemen identified as having died at a relatively young age, even for the era are:

Charles Scrivens (Little Mill) died in late 1918 aged 40 following his medical discharge with tuberculosis: Evi Harper (Monkswood) died in 1920 aged 31: Arthur Philips (Goytre Wharf) died in 1923 aged 33: Valentine Morris (Penperlleni) died in 1928 aged 41: George Bandfield (Nantyderry) died in 1931 aged 42: Lewis Bowen (Mamhilad) also died in 1931 aged 41 and Lewis Brown (Croes y pant) in 1934 aged 43.

However, several of those who survived went on to lead long lives, the oldest discovered during research was Iltyd Charles Jenkins of New Barn Farm, Penperlleni who served in the Royal Engineers. Having moved away from Goytre after the war he died in the Farnborough area in 1991, aged 93.

Goytre Cricket Team 1921. Lionel Whitehead (rear centre) and Albert Higgs (believed to be rear far right), both served with the Monmouthshire Regiment

Like many communities Goytre raised memorials to commemorate its dead and to honour survivors. Due to the dispersed communities that made up Goytre at the time, there was no central memorial; rather each church or chapel had its own plaques or tablets, together with those erected by private individuals or families.

Capel Ed

Built in 1807 and extended in the twentieth century, the chapel contains just two plaques, situated at the far end of the inside of the building.

The first plaque is dedicated to the memory of William John Thomas who had been studying at Trevecca College, Talgarth as a candidate for the Welsh Presbyterian Church, before he enlisted. Born in Cwmavon and educated at Caerleon, William was a gardener on the Llanover Estate before entering Trevecca.

In Memory of Lance Corporal William John Thomas, A Faithful Member of This Church And A Student for the Ministry, Who Died Fighting On The Somme, Oct 6th 1916. Aged 27 years

Above William's plaque is one dedicated to the memory of Llewelyn Thomas Richards, erected by his mother who had been born in Mamhilad.

In Loving Memory of Llewelyn Thomas Richards, 2nd Lieut. Royal Welsh Fusiliers. Killed In Action in France Sept 5th 1918. Age 20 Years. Buried North of Bapaume. Youngest Son Of The Late W.D Richards. Pontllanfraith. And Grandson Of the Late Thomas Thomas. Mamhilad. This Table Is Erected By His Mother. Dulce Et Decorum Est Pro Patria Mori.

Capel Ed Cottages (right), at the rear of the chapel, now used by the Community Garden. Former residents include Goytre soldiers Albert Cotterell and Reginald Cornish

Saron Baptist Chapel

The Chapel was built in 1826 but rebuilt in 1865 to incorporate a school room and gallery. Saron's war memorial, which was unveiled on 8th July 1920, records in order of rank the names of four who were killed and nineteen who returned. Names from the Morgan family feature prominently, whose ancestors gave the land on which the Chapel was built. Two of the four dead were killed serving with overseas forces.

Killed
LCpl David Harry SLI, Pte William Higgs 2nd Mons, Pte Lewis Morgan Cal USA, Pte James Cule NZF

Survived
2ndLts – A Evans MC RFA, B Morgan RFA, E Humphreys Can AF,
Sgts – W Harry Gdn Hgls, W Morgan 2nd Mons, W Thomas 2nd Mons,
Pte D Morgan SWB
LCpls – W Griffiths SWB
Ptes - T Griffiths RFA, Pte G Jones 2nd Mons, Pte L Brown 2nd Mons, Pte C Morgan 2nd Mons, Pte A Higgs 2nd Mons, LCpl I Phillips 2nd Mons, Pte J Rogers RFA, Pte J Hardwick RFA, Pte V Jones 2nd Yorks, Pte I Charles Bdr Regt, A B I Jones HMS Malaya

St Peter's Church

First mentioned in records in 1348 but largely rebuilt in 1846 and enlarged again in 1981, St Peter's contains both a war memorial and two individual plaques. The main memorial comprises of a marble tablet fixed to the wall of the nave and commemorates both casualties and survivors, the names of casualties being highlighted in gold leaf.

The tablet was designed in 1920 by Harry Gregory and, after approval from the parish committee, Henry Durnell worked on the lettering in

January and February 1921. The tablet itself was produced by W. Clarke of Llandaff with the Sicilian marble supplied by Walton, Woody and Cripps of Bristol. The slate frame was made by Sessions & Sons of Cardiff. In all it took 358 man hours to complete at a cost of £52 and was unveiled in May 1921.

A marble memorial tablet in St Peter's also states that oak panelling in the church was installed to remember the fallen. Work started on the panelling in September 1920 and was completed around the same time as the tablet, at a cost of £360.

The memorial commemorates

Killed
R Baker, E J Davies, G Dobbs, J Dobbs, E Evans, H Guest, E Harper, S H Kirby, C E V Knight, E O Morgan, A Parsons

Survived
W C Andrews, G Bandfield, W H Belcher, R Bowen, I Charles, W J Charles, F Collins, R Cornish, A Cotterell, C Cox, E B Cuthbertson, F C Day, T Day
D Edmunds, A Edwards, G Evans, W Evans, G Gwatkin, R Harding, S E Harding, S E Harding, E A Jenkins, I Jenkins, P Jenkins, W J Jenkins, E Lloyd
C W Merrick, B Morris, E Morris, S Morris, V Morris, A Parsons, G Parsons, W Parsons, A T Phillips, F J Phillips, I C Phillips, A Probert, A Powles, R J Rosser, W Summers, L D Whitehead

Church Farm (circa 1550) the home of Gilbert Gwatkin who served with the Labour Corps. He is commemorated as a survivor on the St Peter's memorial

The first individual plaque (below) is dedicated to Walter James Robinson who at the time of his death was engaged to the Rector's daughter-

In Loving Memory of Walter James Robinson. 7ᵗʰ Buffs, Son Of James Robinson. Woodbine House, Pinchbeck, Lincs. Killed In Action In Flanders, October 12ᵗʰ 1917, Aged 37 Years. The Souls Of The Righteous Are In The Hands Of God.

A transcript of letters between the Rector, Joseph Davies and the family of Walter Robinson, following his death are included in Appendix B.

A second plaque remembers Sidney Kirby, killed leading his men in an assault on enemy positions at Gallipoli.

In Loving Memory Of Sidney Henry Kirby 2ⁿᵈ Lieut: 10ᵗʰ Border Regt. Att 1/5ᵗʰ H.L.I. Grandson of Colonel Henry Byrde, Kandy. Killed In Action At Krithia, Nullah, Gallipoli. December 19ᵗʰ 1915 – Aged 24. 'I Am The Resurrection And The Life'.

The Byrde family was connected with Goytre for many generations, from the time that Captain Henry Byrde purchased Goytre House in 1785 until the last of the Byrde descendants to reside there died in 1949. Many Byrdes served as Army Officers and several died on active service, from as far back as the Napoleonic Wars up to as recently as WW2 and Malaya in the 1950s.[1]

Henry, the first Byrde of Goytre House had been serving with the Army in America in the 1770s when he rescued Elizabeth, a young English girl. She had been captured and enslaved by Shoni Indians after they had attacked her family's farm and massacred all apart from her. Henry married Elizabeth and they purchased Goytre House on their return to England. For years the pub sign (left) for the Goytre Arms depicted Henry in his Army uniform with Elizabeth in Native American dress.

Overseas

Goytre's war dead are buried or commemorated across cemeteries on the Western Front and the Middle East. Ernest Morgan is remembered on the famous Menin Gate. William Higgs, who was killed on the first day of the Somme, and David Harry, are listed on the Thiepval memorial for those who fell at the Somme and have no known grave. Another Goytre pair, Walter Robinson and Fred Pinfield, are both commemorated on the Tyne Cot memorial. In the Middle East Sidney

---

[1] Major Henry Byrde (b.1917) of the 1st Battalion, Welsh Regiment died from illness whilst on active service in Malaya in 1957 whilst attached to the Royal Welsh Fusiliers. Cremated in Singapore he has a memorial stone in the church yard at St Peters

Kirby is buried at the Dardanelles and Albert Parsons is remembered on the Basra War Memorial in Southern Iraq.

Two Goytre soldiers, Reginald Baker (below right) and Charles Knight (below left), killed nearly three years apart, are both buried in Poelcapelle cemetery, six miles north east of Ypres in Belgium.

Cefn Mawr Wood, Monkswood (below)

Appendix A – Summary of the Fallen

Name	Date of Death	Age	Buried	Memorial(s)
DAVIES, Edward John	25-Oct 1914	38	No known grave	Ploegsteert Memorial, Belgium. St Peter's
GUEST, Henry	11-Dec 1914	19	Calvaire Military Cemetery, Belgium	St Peter's
BAKER, Reginald Lawrence	8-May 1915	36	Poelcapelle British Cemetery, Belgium	St Peter's and other locations in the Abergavenny area
EVANS, Benjamin	27-Sep 1915	25	No known grave	Loos Memorial, France. Abergavenny Market Hall
KIRBY, Sidney Herbert	19-Dec 1915	24	Pink Farm Cemetery, Gallipoli, Turkey	St Peter's
PARSONS, Albert Victor	9-Apr 1916	20	No known grave	Basra Memorial, Iraq. St Peter's
HIGGS, William Thomas	1-Jul 1916	22	No known grave	Thiepval Memorial, France. Saron Baptist
DOBBS, George	27-Jul 1916	23	Sucrerie Military Cemetery, France	St Peter's
HARRY, David	30-Aug 1916	27	No known grave	Thiepval Memorial, France. St Peter's
CULE, James Aaron	15-Sep 1916	27	Serre Road No2 Cemetery, France	Saron Baptist
THOMAS, William John	6-Oct 1916	27	Doullens Communal Cemetery, France	Capel Ed, Christchurch (Newport)
MORGAN, Ernest Oliver	20-Jun 1917	36	No known grave	Menin Gate, Belgium St Peter's. Boddington, Australia
PINFIELD, Frederick Bertram	29-Sep 1917	36	No known grave	Tyne Cot Memorial, Belgium. Chippenham War Memorial
ROBINSON,	12-Oct 1917	37	No known grave	St Peter's.

Walter James				Tyne Cot Memorial, Belgium. Newport Athletic Club
KNIGHT, Charles Ernest Vickery	10-Mar 1918	19	Poelcapelle British Cemetery, Belgium	St Peter's
LEWIS, Percy Thomas	2-Jul 1918	22	Varennes Cemetery, France	
DOBBS, John Arthur	6-Jul 1918	18	Bagneux Cemetery, France	St Peter's
RICHARDS, Llewellyn Thomas	5-Sep 1918	20	Morval Cemetery, France	Capel Ed
MORGAN, Lewis Earl	26-Sep 1918	28	Unknown	Saron Baptist
EVANS, E	Unknown		Unknown	St Peter's

Woodland above Byrgwm Mawr, the home of Benjamin Evans, killed in action serving with the Welsh Guards in 1915.

Appendix B – The Walter Robinson Letters

Born in Lincolnshire, Walter James Robinson is recorded on the 1911 census as a bank clerk boarding at 51 Risca Road, Newport. Working for Lloyd's Bank he was also engaged to Muriel, the daughter of the Revd. Joseph Davies of St Peter's Church.

Serving with the 7th Battalion, East Kent Regiment, Walter was killed in action on 12th October 1917. With no known grave, Walter is commemorated on the Tyne Cot memorial, Newport Athletic Club memorial and at St Peter's Church.

During research for this book the church came forward and shared the following letters between the Davies and the Robinson families in the aftermath of Walter's death.

Dearest Betty

Your letter came this morning telling us the sad news – one hardly knows what to say, words are so unable to express what one feels or would like to say – your poor dear people – I can't tell you how we feel for you and what it means to us too – All who knew or had anything to do with 'Romp' must I think feel the same and I know how dear old Willie will feel it and what he thought of him. It will be hard telling him for I shan't see him till tonight. It seems so difficult to understand why those things are allowed to be – I know too how brave you will be dear Betty and the one to cheer the others up – I used to notice that at Leicester, whatever troubles you had you always had a cheery word for "lame dogs" – I will not write anymore now, but I am sure you will know how much we feel for you and if there was anything one could do, we would do it.

My God bless and comfort you all.

Ever your loving friend

Muriel

The Rectory

Goytrey
Nr Abergavenny
Mon

My Dear Mrs Robinson

The terribly sad news came to us this morning that your gallant and dear son had been killed in action on the 12th Oct, his friend Mr Williams wrote and told me. Muriel has just been told and is terribly cut up. To you – his parents and sisters – we offer our deepest sympathy in your great loss of a good son. I believe him to have been a good and true man, and I shall always remember his deep attachment to my daughter. She has lost a noble man and she has I feel sure your full sympathy. We were all so looking forward to his leave – but God willed otherwise! My heart is too full to write more now. With fullest and deepest sympathy and our prayers that God may comfort you all and Muriel in this hour of trial.

I am – yours very sincerely

Joseph Davies

My Dear Miss R

We do sincerely hope that you are all bearing up bravely in this dark hour of trial and sorrow. It was only on one occasion that I had the privilege of meeting dear Walter and that was when he came up here one Sunday last year. I liked him then; and when he wrote me in Sept I had no hesitation in giving my consent to the engagement. I shall always treasure the 2 letters and pc I received from him – the letters were so honest and straight forward – It is so heart rending to think that he has passed away before I had received his last letter. He was one of the gallant band who defended with themselves the liberty which is dearer than life: the honour which is dearer than earthly existence – sorrow is in every case mingled with pride. We lift up our heads – we cannot see light so long as we look at our loss – as we lift up our heads we seem to see the Saviour smile. His purpose of regeneration is being worked out. The gift of our dear brave Walter has been part of the purpose. Sadness will always be our lot upon earth but as we look up light will shine upon us. Days and months and years of life lie before us perhaps before we shall meet dear Walter again in the great beyond. But we must always thank Him that we have been allowed in Walters's sacrifice to take part in His great purpose for the cleansing of the world.

94

He was a brave conscientious man who counted not his life dear unto himself and I shall respect his memory always for his deep attachment to Muriel and for being a good and true man. In the midst of this great sorrow we must still trust God to say with Whittier " Yet in the maddening maze of things and tossed by storm and flood. To one fixed trust my spirit clings. I know that God is good." My dear Muriel was very anxious to go to you and we could not oppose her wish under the sad circumstances I hope she is a comfort to you as I know you are all to her – I pray that the Giver of gifts may bless and comfort you and yours now and always.

With kindest regards

Yours very sincerely

Joseph Davies

9-11-17
Dear Miss R

Very many thanks for the paper read this am. I hope you are all bearing up bravely as I last saw you. Muriel went to the bank on Wed am. She is very quiet not like her usual self – Did you have any definite news from Williams, if so, please let us know and also any information you may get from the W.O. I had been hoping there was still a possibility that dear Walter was still alive but now I have given up all hope of seeing him on this side. He did his duty nobly and gallantly on the battlefield and his rest is well earned. "May he rest in peace" You have all been very much in my thoughts since I left you and once again "thank you" for your extreme kindness to M and myself. While life remains, there will be a link between us in memory of him whom we mourn. I can assure you that he is sincerely mourned in this house. That God may strengthen you all to bear your heavy burden is my earnest prayer.

With kindest regards to you all.

I am yours very sincerely

Joseph Davies

The Rectory

Goytrey

Dear Miss Robinson

It was kind of you to write me that nice letter in all your trouble – I am sorry from the depths of my heart for your dear Father and Mother, yourself and your sister. My husband and I had got to look upon your dear brother as one of ourselves although it is not often that we met. Muriel would show us his letters from time to time and we felt satisfied that our child was given to a man of Stirling worth – brave and true and one who would be a husband to her in the truest sense. But it was not to be, it is hard to see the wisdom of it but He knows best and we must try and be resigned to His will. I hope our darling Muriel will be a little comfort to you all. When no letter came from you yesterday she hesitated then said "I will go". My love and deepest sympathy to you all and Believe me – yours very sincerely

A.S. Davies

St Peter's Church. At the time of the Great War the church was under the stewardship of the Rector Joseph Davies, whose daughter was engaged to Walter Robinson. Walter was killed in action in 1917.

96

Appendix C – Summary of Units

Army

Army Cycling Corps (1 served)

MORGAN, Clifford Louis. 19977, Private [Later Army Service Corps]

Army Pay Corps (1 served)

MORGAN, John William. 8088, Corporal

Army Service Corps (3 served)

EDWARDS, Albert. T4/274871, Private.

JENKINS, Edward Albert. M/152023

TURFREY, John. M2/203289, Private

Border Regiment (2 served, 1 died)

CHARLES, Isaac Jenkins. 33701, Private, 1st Battalion

KIRBY, Sidney Henry. Second Lieutenant, 10th Battalion. KILLED IN ACTION

Cavalry (1 served)

ALEXANDER, Frank. 39620, Private, 3rd Hussars

Gordon Highlanders (1 served)

HARRY, William. 10029, Sergeant, 1st Battalion. PRISONER OF WAR

King's Liverpool Regiment (2 served)

MORGAN, Alfred. 91476, Private, 4th Battalion. WOUNDED

PHILLIPS, Arthur Thomas. 73723, Private [Later 49539 Labour Corps]

King's Royal Rifle Corps (1 served, 1 died)

PINFIELD, Frederick Bertram. R/38020, Lance Corporal, 13th Battalion. KILLED IN ACTION

King's Shropshire Light Infantry (2 served, 2 died)

DAVIES, Edward John. 7480, Private, 1st Battalion. KILLED IN ACTION

HARRY, David. 17342. Lance Corporal, 5th Battalion, KILLED IN ACTION

Labour Corps (4 served)

EDMUNDS, Daniel. 39572, Private, Agricultural Company

GWATKIN, Gilbert. 290800, Private, Agricultural Company

HARDING, Richard. 1701814. Private, Agricultural Company

SUMMERS, William John. Private

Machine Gun Corps (2 served, 2 died)

DOBBS, John Arthur. 154127, Private. KILLED IN ACTION [also served Loyal North Lancashire Regt]

THOMAS, William John. 31176, Lance Corporal. DIED OF WOUNDS

Monmouthshire Regiment (21 served, 3 died)

BAKER, Reginald Lawrence. Captain, 3rd Battalion. KILLED IN ACTION

BROWN, Lewis. 1916, Private, 2nd Battalion

CLARK, James. 1349, Private, 2nd Battalion

CORNISH, Reginald. 1343, Private, 2nd Battalion

COTTERELL, Albert H. W., 3153, Private, 2nd Battalion

CUTHBERTSON CMG MVO OBE, Edward B. Lieutenant Colonel, 2nd Battalion

DAVIS, Jack. 2015, Private, 1st Battalion [Later 670005 Labour Corps]

GUEST, Henry. 1345, Private, 2nd Battalion. KILLED IN ACTION

HIGGS, Albert Edward. 3164, 2nd Battalion

HIGGS, William Thomas. 1344, Privatem 2nd Battalion. KILLED IN ACTION

JAMES, John David. 3910 [Later 266772 Welsh Regiment]

JONES, G. Private, 2nd Battalion

MORGAN, William. 2288, Sergeant, 2nd Battalion

PHILLIPS, Ivor Charles. 3382, Private, 2nd Battalion

SKILLERN, George Henry. 1334, Private, 2nd Battalion

SKILLERN, William Thomas. 1337, Private, 2nd Battalion

THOMAS, William. 266023, Lance Sergeant, 1st Battalion

THOMAS, W. Sergeant, 2nd Battalion

WALL MSM, Frank Edward. 1339, WOII, 2nd Battalion

WILLIAMS, Arthur J. 265700, Private, 2nd Battalion

WHITEHEAD, Lionel Digby. Captain, 3rd Battalion

Royal Army Medical Corps (3 served)

EMERY, Thomas. 78039, Acting Corporal, No 84 Casualty Clearing Station

JONES, William. 5818, Private, 14 General Hospital

PHILLIPS, Major Herbert. 266096, Corporal

Royal Engineers (6 served)

BOWEN, Lewis Richard. 213542, Sapper [briefly served with the Durham Light Infantry]

EVANS, James Thomas. 108185, Driver, 124 Field Company, Welsh Division

JENKINS, Iltyd Charles. WR/22221, Corporal, Railway Company

JENKINS, William John. 260095

SMITH, James. 51791, Sapper

WILLIAMS, Alfred. 1874, Lance Corporal, Royal Monmouthshire Royal Engineers

Royal Field Artillery (8 served)

COWLES, John George

EVANS MC, Arthur Edward. Lieutenant - WOUNDED

GRIFFITHS, T.

JAMES, John. 214703, Gunner

LLOYD, Edward Arthur. 214725, Gunner

MORGAN, Benjamin. Lieutenant

ROSSER, William George. 43990, Gunner

SKILLERN, Charles. 190729, Gunner

Royal Garrison Artillery (2 served)

WALL, George Wilfred. 199378, Gunner

WALTON, George. 186020, Gunner

Royal Welsh Fusiliers (4 served, 2 died)

MORGAN, Richard H. 77331, Private.

PARSONS, Albert Victor. 13841, Lance Corporal, 8th Battalion - KILLED IN ACTION

PHILLIPS, Charles. 75010, Private, 5th Battalion

RICHARDS, Llewellyn Thomas. Lieutenant, 17th Battalion - KILLED IN ACTION

South Lancashire Regiment (2 served)

GOODWIN, William. 266503, Private, 14th Battalion

WESTLAKE, Ernest James. 61780, Private, 16th Battalion

South Wales Borderers (14 served, 3 died)

DAY, Thomas. 3nd Battalion

DOBBS, George. 21419, Private, 10th Battalion - KILLED IN ACTION

GRIFFITHS, William John. 3509, 1/1 (Brecknock Battalion)

HARPER, Evi. 22002, Private, 11th Battalion

JENKINS, Phillip. 15257, Private, 1st Battalion [later 33888 1st Battalion Royal Welsh Fusiliers]

JONES, Edwin James. 46825, Private, 1st Battalion [also 170th Tunnelling Company]

KNIGHT, Charles Ernest Vickery. 41349, Private, 2nd Battalion - KILLED IN ACTION

MORGAN, Ira Charles. 14496, Private 7th and 12 Battalions

LEWIS, Percy Thomas. 31083, Lance Corporal, 10th Battalion - KILLED IN ACTION

MORGAN, David Hugh

PHILLIPS, James France, Private, 3rd Battalion [Later Labour Corps]

POWLES, Arthur William. 30075, Private, 4th Battalion

SCRIVENS, Charles. 36701, Private

STINCHCOMBE, George Francis. 22457, Private, 11th Battalion [Later Lance Corporal, 156321, Royal Engineers]

Tank Corps (1 served)

BRINKWORTH, William John. 111685, Private, 7th Battalion

Welsh Guards (2 served, 1 died)

EVANS, Benjamin. 1348, Guardsman, 1st Battalion - KILLED IN ACTION

WILLIAMS, Ernest E. 2990, Guardsman, 2nd Battalion

Welsh Regiment (6 served)

GUPPY, John Henry. 54014, Private. [Later 629652 Labour Corps & Royal Defence Corps]

JENKINS, ARTHUR. 46948, Private, 1st Battalion

JONES, William Robert. 48225, Private

LLOYD, Jonah Henry. 27761, Private, 18th Battalion

MORRIS, Valentine Evan. 52777, Private, 1st Battalion

ROSSER, Robert John. 52854, Private 8th Battalion

Worcestershire Regiment (1 served)

BACHE, Sidney. 1975, Private, [Later 435637, Royal Army Medical Corps]

Yorkshire Regiment (1 served)

JONES, Vernon. 9726, Private, 2/4th Battalion

Royal Navy (1 served)

JONES, Ivor David. Z/2839, Able Seaman, HMS Malaya

Royal Flying Corps / Royal Air Force (2 served)

BANDFIELD, George. 167709, Corporal

BROWN, Arthur. 119654, Private

Merchant Navy (1 served)

JONES, Evan. Master Mariner

Overseas Forces (6 served, 3 died)

CULE, James Aaron. 23/1960, Private. New Zealand Rifle Brigade. KILLED IN ACTION

HUMPHREYS, Ernest, 2nd Lieutenant. Canadian Forces

MORGAN, Azariah Decimus. United States Army

MORGAN, Ernest Oliver. 1896, Private. Australian Imperial Force. KILLED IN ACTION

MORGAN, Lewis Earl. Private, 364th Infantry, 91st Division, United States Army. KILLED IN ACTION

MORGAN, Ulysses Grant. United States Army

Commemorative bench, Little Mill remembering both the outbreak of the Great War and the D-Day Landings.

Little Mill, with Folly Tower in the background

Appendix D - Medals of the Great War

This section describes the medals awarded for service in the Great War that are mentioned in this book. Several Goytre veterans had been previously decorated for service in the Boer War; these are noted in their biographies where known, however descriptions of them have not been included as that conflict is outside the scope of this publication.

Military Cross
A third level gallantry award instituted in December 1914 for commissioned officers[1] in recognition of gallantry in operations against the enemy. Initially also awarded for meritorious service, the criteria was soon updated to cover only acts of bravery.

Meritorious Service Medal
Awarded since 1845 to non-commissioned officers for distinguished service or gallantry not in the face of the enemy. When not awarded for gallantry it was used to reward individuals of good, faithful and meritorious service who also had irreproachable conduct.

1914 Star
Authorised in 1917 and awarded for service in France or Belgium between 5th August and midnight on 22nd/23rd November 1914, the date the First Battle of Ypres ended. A clasp was instituted in 1919 and granted to those who during the qualifying period had served under fire or were within range of enemy artillery.

1914/15 Star
Instituted in December 1918 and granted to those who served in France or Belgium between 23rd th August 1914 and 31st December 1915 or had served in any other operational theatre from 5th August 1914.

---

[1] Non-Commissioned Ranks were eligible for the award of the Military Medal for similar acts. The same system applied to the award of the Distinguished Service Order / Distinguished Conduct Medal and several other decorations. This two-tier system was scrapped following the 1993 Honours System Review led by then Prime Minister, John Major.

British War Medal

Instituted in July 1919 for those who served on active duty during the war. This time period was later extended to cover operations in Russia up to 1920. Qualifying zones differed between service. Soldiers had to have completed 28 days service and either entered a theatre of operations or an overseas territory. The Royal Air Force used the same criteria as the Army but extended eligibility to those who had seen combat whilst flying from UK bases. The Navy awarded the medal to those who completed 28 days service but did not require them to have served overseas. Merchant Seaman qualified for the medal if they served at sea for no less than six months and had completed one or more voyages through a danger zone.

Mercantile Marine War Medal

Established in 1919 by the Board of Trade and awarded to all those who between 4th August 1914 and 11th November 1918 completed one or more voyages through a danger zone or service at sea for no less than six months.

Victory Medal

Awarded to those who entered a theatre of operation during the war, including airmen engaged in combat flying from UK bases. Many Territorial Force Soldiers who served on garrison duty in India and did not enter a theatre of war only received the British War Medal. Those who were mentioned in dispatches during the war received an oakleaf emblem to wear on their Victory Medal ribbon.

(Left) Medal group comprising of the 1914/15 Star, British War Medal and Victory Medal. A common group amongst Great War veterans, indicating service in an operational theatre some time between the start of the war and 31st December 1915.

Photograph Acknowledgements

Apart from where cited below, photographs were taken by either the author or Richard Dowle.

Photograph of Frederick Pinfield. Cover and page 59. Used with the permission of John Belcher, http://www.pro-patria.co.uk/

Photograph of Charles Merrick. Cover. Used with the permission of Brenda Harris

Photograph of Percy Lewis. Cover and page 45. Image provided by Mike Jones, original source unknown.

Photograph of William and Billy Morgan. Cover and page 54. Used with the permission of Jeff & Jane Phillips

Photograph of the Poppies & Goytre Arms. Page 1. Used with the permission of David Owen.

Photograph of the Carpenter's Arms. Page 4. Used with the permission of David Owen, from his father's photograph collection

Photograph of the School Lane. Page 5. Used with the permission of David Owen, from his father's photograph collection

Photograph of Rose, Ivy and Phoenix Cottages, Penperlleni. Page 6. Used with the permission of Allan Otton

Photograph of the 2nd Monmouthshire Regiment. Page 10. Used with the permission of the Torfaen Trust

Photograph of Edward Cuthbertson. Page 25. Image supplied by David Nicholas, author of 'They Fought With Pride'

Photograph of Mametz Welsh Division Memorial. Page 28. Used with the permission of Angela Jones

Photograph of Henry Guest. Page 33. Image supplied by David Nicholas, author of 'They Fought With Pride'

Photograph of William Thomas Higgs. Page 38. Image supplied by David Nicholas, author of 'They Fought With Pride'

Photograph of John David James. Page 39. Used with the permission of the family

Photograph of Charles Merrick. Page 47. Used with the permission of Brenda Harris

Photograph of Azariah Morgan and sons. Page 49. Used with the permission of Jeff & Jane Phillips

Photograph of Ira Morgan. Page 52. Used with the permission of the family

Photograph of Pinfield Lane. Page 61. Used with the permission of John Belcher, http://www.pro-patria.co.uk/

Photograph of Walter Robinson. Page 63. Used with the permission of Goytre Church

Photograph of Frank Wall. Page 70. Image supplied by David Nicholas, author of 'They Fought With Pride'

Photograph of Lionel Whitehead. Page 72. Used with the permission of David Owen, from his father's photograph collection

Photograph of the Edgar Thomas. Page 79. Used with the permission of Gwyneth Stratten

Photograph of the Old Smithy, Penperlleni. Page 79. Used with the permission of Allan Otton

Photograph of Goytre School. Page 80. Used with the permission of David Owen, from his father's photograph collection

Photograph of Goytre Cricket Club, 1921. Page 83. Used with the permission of David Owen, from his father's photograph collection

Photograph of the Saron Chapel War Memorial. Page 86. Used with the permission of Saron Baptist Chapel

Photograph of Goytre Arms sign. Page 89. Used with the permission of David Owen

Photograph of Charles Knight's grave. Page 90. Used with the permission of the photographer, Angela Jones

Photograph of Reginald Baker's grave. Page 90. Used with the permission of the photographer, Angela Jones

Sources

Online

Abergavenny First World War Memorials:
http://historypoints.org/index.php?page=abergavenny-war-memorial-fww

Australian Service Records:
http://www.naa.gov.au/collection/explore/defence/service-records/army-wwi.aspx

British Army Service Records 1914-1920:
https://search.ancestry.co.uk/search/db.aspx?dbid=1219

British Army Pension Records 1914-1920:
https://search.ancestry.co.uk/search/db.aspx?dbid=1114

Census Records
https://www.ancestry.co.uk/search/categories/35/

Chippenham War Memorial Website:
http://www.pro-patria.co.uk/

Commonwealth War Graves Commission:
https://www.cwgc.org/

Ellis Island Immigration Records:
https://www.libertyellisfoundation.org/passenger

Goetre and Llanover Churches Website:
http://www.goetre-llanover-churches.btck.co.uk/

Goytre Community Council Website:
http://www.community-council.org.uk/goetrefawr/

Goytre Local History Website (Viv Rosser):
http://www.goytrelocalhistory.org.uk/

London Gazette:
https://www.thegazette.co.k/

MonGenes
http://www.mongenes.org.uk/Home.html

Monmouthshire Warriors (Shaun McGuire)
http://www.shaunmcguire.co.uk/

Royal Air Force Airmen's Service Records 1912-1939:
https://search.findmypast.co.uk/search-world-records/british-royal-air-force-airmens-service-records-1912-1939

Saron Baptist Chapel
http://our-uk.co.uk/Saron-Baptist.htm

School Admission Registers (1870-1914):
https://www.findmypast.co.uk/school-registers

Soldiers Died in The Great War:
https://search.ancestry.co.uk/search/db.aspx?dbid=1543

UK Railway Employment Records 1833-1956:
https://search.ancestry.co.uk/search/db.aspx?dbid=1728

Welsh Guards 1914-1918:
https://search.findmypast.co.uk/search-world-records/welsh-guards-1914-1918

Welsh Newspapers Online:
https://newspapers.library.wales/

WW1 Medal Index Cards:
https://search.ancestry.co.uk/search/db.aspx?dbid=1262

Offline

Broadhead, R. 2010. The Great War Chippenham Soldiers: O&B Services

Dixon, J, Dixon J. 2000. Out Since 14: Abertillery, Old Bakehouse Publications

Dixon, J, Dixon J. 1991. With Rifle And Pick: Cardiff, Cwm Press

Dixon, J, Hughes, L. 1995. Surrender Be Damned: Cardiff, Cwm Press

Lloyd, W.G. 1995. Roll Of Honour: Cwmbran, W.G Lloyd

Nicholas, D. 2005. They Fought With Pride: Cwmbran, Nicholas Publishing

Somerset, W.H.B., Tyler H.G., Whitehead L.D[1]. 1926. On the Western Front 1/3rd Monmouthshire Regiment: Usk, Sergeant Brothers

Westlake, R. 2001. First World War Graves and Memorials In Gwent Volume 1: Barnsley, Wharncliffe Books

Westlake, R. 2002. First World War Graves and Memorials In Gwent Volume 2: Barnsley, Wharncliffe Books

Tribute at Wellacre, Penperlleni on 100th Anniversary of the end of the Great War

---

[1] Lionel Digby Whitehead of Goytre Hall, officer of the 3rd Mons during the Great War

Made in the USA
Monee, IL
11 August 2021

75394483R00069